# HEALING ANOINTING

# HEALING ANOINTING

## Hope for a hurting world

Colin Dye

# Hodder & Stoughton

LONDON SYDNEY AUCKLAND

First published in Great Britain in 1997
by Hodder and Stoughton
A division of Hodder Headline PLC

1 3 5 7 9 10 8 6 4 2

British Library Cataloguing in Publication Data
A record for this book is available from the British Library

ISBN 0 340 67866 6

Typeset by Avon Dataset Ltd, Bidford-on-Avon, Warks

Printed and bound in Great Britain by
Clays Ltd, St Ives plc

Hodder and Stoughton
A division of Hodder Headline PLC
338 Euston Road
London NW1 3BH

To Laura, whose healing is complete in Jesus

# CONTENTS

# 1

# THE GOD WHO HEALS

1 believe that Yahweh, the living God of Israel, has been a healing God throughout the whole of human history, that he is still the great physician today, and that he will be my full and perfect healer at the last day of resurrection. This deep, abiding, personal belief is based on both revelation and observation, on what I read in the Bible and on what I regularly see in Britain and abroad.

In Exodus 15:26, God personally identified and introduced himself to the people of Israel as Yahweh Rapha, the Lord who heals you. This divine revelation came at a critical time for the Jews as God had just liberated them from slavery in Egypt and helped them to cross the Red Sea. Just three days later, when they were facing their first test and their first doubts in the wilderness, God revealed his healing name and nature to them.

Exodus 15:22–27 is a pivotal passage for it records the first law and the first promise that God gave to Israel after leaving Egypt. In many ways, the revelation of God as healer is the introduction to all the detailed rules of the Mosaic Law and establishes the therapeutic principle behind all the regulations which follow.

Luke 4:16–20 reports a similar divine revelation at the beginning of Jesus' ministry. Immediately after he had passed through the waters of baptism and survived his encounter in the wilderness with the enemy, he also personally introduced himself to Israel as the one who was 'sent to heal'.

Everything that follows, in both the Old and the New Testaments, is built upon these two revelations that healing is fundamental to the nature of the Father and the Son – and at the heart of their dealings with their people. God is revealed as a healer right through the Scriptures, from Abimelech to Eutychus, from Genesis to Acts, and on in the days foreseen in the book of Revelation. Even without the considerable testimony of believers today and through the ages, the weight of scriptural evidence is enough to convince me that the God I love and serve is the great healer.

Yet, nearly every Sunday, I also see convincing proof in my London congregation that God is still Yahweh Rapha today. A thick pile of testimonies lies on my desk which vividly describes how God has brought some degree of healing to a large number of our members in the last few years. Seeing all this, it seems eminently reasonable for me to conclude that our healing God can be relied upon to carry on healing in and through his people right up to the day of resurrection.

I also believe that God has implanted a natural, human desire for health, healing and wholeness in all his children, everywhere. Even in our cynical, post-modern age, hurting people are turning in increasing numbers to a growing array of counsellors, complementary medical practitioners, alternative therapists and psychic healers – as well as to their local doctors and nurses. Quite simply, wherever I travel in the world, people are hungry for healing, and they will go to anyone who offers it, no matter how cranky or dangerous. Therefore, it seems vital that the Church should be unashamedly open in proclaiming the truth that our loving, gracious God is the ultimate, compassionate, all-powerful, perfect healer.

Throughout the centuries, the Christian Church has always prayed for the sick and cared for the ill and dying. In most parts of the world, it is the Church which has pioneered and developed basic medical care – often at immense personal sacrifice – as one part of its mission to reveal God's love and grace to the world. The story of Christian hospices and medical missions through the ages – and of modern missionary nurses in less-developed nations – is one of the great hidden glories of the Church. There have always been those sections of the Church, however, which have been concerned to point out that God not only heals through natural processes, hygienic practices and medical remedies, but that he is also willing to intervene personally and heal people supernaturally.

Church history shows that healing 'miracles' have been part of the gospel in most ages, on every continent, and in all traditions. These miracles, however, seem to have been most prevalent during times of revival and great evangelistic zeal, and have been commonly seen among ordinary people who had previously had little contact with the Church.

The ministry of healing has never had a higher profile in the Church than during the twentieth century. Within many Christian traditions there has been a massive surge in interest in a sacramental approach to healing which has stressed the laying on of hands and anointing with holy oil, especially within the context of the Eucharist or communion service.

The first half of the century in Britain saw the emergence of groups like the Guild of Health, the Divine Healing Mission, the Guild of St Raphael, the 1930 Lambeth Conference, the Churches' Council for Health and Healing, and the 1953 Archbishops' Commission on the Church's Ministry of Healing. Through these groups – and a glut of books about divine healing – a large number of traditional church leaders gained an awareness of God's concern for healing.

But the world-wide Christian rediscovery of divine healing in the twentieth century is mainly due to the fast-growing Pentecostal movement. The Pentecostal emphasis on faith and the 1 Corinthians 12 gifts of the Spirit has had an incalculable impact on the Church around the world. Looking back, we can see that God has used people like George and Stephen Jeffries, William Branham, Smith Wigglesworth and Kathryn Kuhlman to reawaken the Church to the miraculous to a degree which they might never have believed possible in their lifetimes.

The charismatic renewal in the last third of the twentieth century built upon Pentecostal teaching and helped the idea of supernatural healing to become more widely accepted. Fountain Trust conferences in the late sixties and early seventies, followed by John Wimber's conferences in the mid-eighties, encouraged many church leaders to try to incorporate divine healing into the pattern of their church life.

3

At the same time, Pentecostal missions, led by men like George Canty with established 'healing ministries', helped a new generation of young leaders to develop a biblical passion for healing and preaching. Throughout the last thirty years, though, most British leaders have been uncomfortably aware that their experience of God's healing power has been only a pale shadow of their counterparts' experience in Africa, Asia and Latin America.

During the last ten years, I have been privileged to minister regularly in parts of the world where the Church is growing the fastest and where healing miracles are far more common than in Britain. The church that I lead in London has benefited from this and we too have experienced considerable growth and are being increasingly blessed in the area of the miraculous. Furthermore, many of our ten thousand members come from the African, Latin American and Asian communities in London, and they have greatly enriched our life and mission with their expectancy and their openness to the supernatural elements of Christian worship and ministry.

Of course, I recognise that miraculous, physical healing is not the totality of the Church's ministry of healing, for we are called to take the healing of the cross to every section of our sick society, not just to people with broken bodies.

I also realise that miraculous healing is only one part of the full health and wholeness which is God's will for us all. I strongly believe, however, that supernatural, physical healing has an important place in New Testament based evangelism – it is a sign which endorses the content of our preaching and points people to the risen Lord Jesus.

It is my commitment to developing a style and pattern of New Testament evangelism which has concentrated this book's focus on the miraculous aspect of healing. At our church, the whole congregation is united in trying to reach the people of London with relevant, radical and effective evangelism which reconciles people with each other and the healing God. It is my hope that by the time you reach the last page of this book, you will also be eager to partner God in his dynamic healing mission to our hurting world.

Although this book may appear to be about miraculous

healing, it is really a book about the healing Father, the healing cross of Jesus, the anointing with the Spirit which equips us for God's healing work – and about the special hope each healing miracle provides. No matter how wonderful any particular healing may be, it is always only a sign pointing towards a far more important reality.

Every divine healing is a signpost which directs hurting people towards the power and love and presence of the all-healing God. Every miraculous healing is a dim foreshadowing that provides a glimpse of the total transformation at the final day which awaits all true believers. And every healing is a sign of the cross that reminds us of Calvary's ultimate healing which made perfect wholeness possible for all people.

Too many believers appear to be more interested in healing than in their heavenly healer. It is as though they would rather stop and admire the signposts than press on to the goal! When I am travelling on a long journey, I depend on a good road map and a reliable navigator to help me find the way. With these two aids I could probably make it to my destination without any signposts. But we all know how encouraging it is to see a sign which shows that we are on the right road and getting closer to our destination. We all watch out for road signs, but very few of us are obsessed with them!

It is the same in the spiritual realm. We have been given God's word and God's Spirit to guide and direct us home, and many believers rightly think that they can manage quite nicely with just these. But our gracious Father also provides us with miraculous signs – with tokens of his love and tastes of his power – to reassure and encourage us on our journey home. It is as foolish to ignore or belittle them as it is to collect them or confuse them with our destination.

In the first two parts of this book, I look back on my own experience and the Scriptures to show that God does heal, and to consider *how* and *why* he heals. In the third part, I look at many of the issues and questions which we need to address today as we seek to minister God's healing in a sceptical world. And in the final part of the book, I look forward and offer some practical suggestions as to how we can become effective healing partners with God.

The prayer of the threatened and censured disciples, in Acts 4:29–30, seems increasingly appropriate to the Church in Europe today. There are many who, like the Jewish religious leaders of that day, are doing their utmost to silence the gospel by opposing divine healing. We cannot do better than pray the disciples' prayer. 'Now, Lord, look on their threats, and grant to your servants that with all boldness they may speak your word, by stretching out your hand to heal, and that signs and wonders may be done through the name of your holy servant Jesus.'

# Part One

## Looking Back

# 2

# NYOTA FARM

As I look back, one experience of God's healing power stands out in my memory as the moment when God finally convinced me about his healing ministry and challenged me to partner him. It did not take place when I was preaching to thousands in a packed and brilliantly lit auditorium, but rather when I was talking to a small handful in a dingy African hut.

I had flown into Kenya determined to pray for people to be healed. It was my first long trip away from my church in London, and I felt free to experiment, to be bold, to make mistakes, to preach and to pray in a way which guaranteed that I would look ridiculous unless God honoured my words. I knew that I would be away from my congregation for nearly three weeks and was determined to give it everything! On the plane I consoled myself with the thought that – if I did make a complete fool of myself – at least I would not have to face these people every Sunday for the following six months.

It was September 1987, and I had seen God heal many people in the previous few years – but mostly through other ministers and other church leaders. I was in my early thirties. I had been a Christian minister for eight years, an assistant minister at Kensington Temple for two years, and I was eager to do what I had not really done before. I wanted to speak God's words of healing and see people healed, clearly healed, not just headaches eased and indigestion improving, but deaf ears hearing, blind eyes opening, lame legs leaping. Nobody could have been more earnest.

I felt good about the trip from the day I accepted the invitation to hold meetings in rural Kenya. Whatever happened spiritually, it was bound to be a special time for me as it was my first visit there in thirty years – I had been born in Kenya, and was going to preach in Nakuru where my father grew up.

Some of the modern realities of Africa quickly brought my three companions and me crashing down to earth. When we arrived in Nairobi as a team, there was no transport and no equipment awaiting us. We had planned to show the 'Jesus' film in the two local languages of Swahili and Kikuyu, but no arrangements had been made. The local leaders who had invited us were neither wealthy nor well organised, so we chased round Nairobi ourselves and hired ancient, crackly, beaten-up versions of the equipment we needed.

We drove north-west in a hired van to Nakuru, and set ourselves up in the town square of its poorest suburb. Each evening, several hundred people gathered in the square to sing. Local pastors and evangelists led the meetings and testified. I preached a simple message, appealed for people to give their lives to Jesus, and – with a fluttering stomach – offered to pray for the sick.

I had not been in a situation quite like this before, and could not tell what was happening. The people whom I prayed for were dreadfully polite: they all said, 'Thank you,' and insisted that they were feeling much better. I assumed that they were merely being nice to a foreign visitor! Yet, when I reviewed the meetings after a few days with the team, we realised that there had been a strong manifestation of healing improvements. We could not say that medical miracles had taken place on the previous evenings, but there had been an awful lot of excited Africans bending and stretching and beaming with glee.

My boldness grew, and at the last meeting in Nakuru I preached on the healing power of Jesus. A twelve-year-old girl was first in the queue when I finally got round to inviting sick people forward for prayer. Her companions told us that she had been deaf and dumb from birth. Without thinking, I found myself announcing, 'She shall hear and speak!' The team stared at me in astonishment, but I was even more surprised than they were – for I had not said anything like it before in eight years of ministry.

We prayed for the girl, then I stood behind her and called

her by name. Nothing happened. The team evangelist joined me and clapped his hands. The girl turned round and started to speak – not well or clearly, but falteringly, like someone learning to talk. It was a wonderful moment.

We visited the girl at a local house on the following day. Everyone was delighted, for she was hearing and speaking words much more clearly. The real joy was that she had been brought to Nakuru from the countryside to start attending a deaf school. I learnt later that she never did go there!

Excited, we left that family and were taken a few streets away to visit a bedridden woman in a typical two-room house. The team and I were elated after talking with the girl, and did not grasp how seriously ill this woman was. We approached the house chattering about the girl, but became aware of an incredible spiritual atmosphere as soon as we went inside. We could feel that the sovereign God was standing in that tiny home beside us. We prayed for the woman, who was bedridden with a serious heart condition. She got up, started dancing round the room, and promptly gave her life to Jesus. Everyone was overjoyed. None of us had experienced anything like it before.

From Nakuru, we drove high up to the mountains of the Rift Valley for some meetings at a place called Nyota Farm. This was to be our base for a few days, and we went out from there to nearby farms, speaking in the fields to groups of about thirty or forty people at a time. We preached, urged the farm workers and their families to follow Jesus, and offered to pray for the sick. There were several healings and a clear sense of power in evangelism; many people accepted Jesus. Then a group asked us to pray for a boy with a withered leg who looked as though he was suffering from polio.

About two dozen curious Africans crowded round us. We prayed and prayed until we ran out of words and energy. Eventually, crestfallen, we gave up. The young boy limped off in the same way that he had limped up, and we drove back to the farm feeling as useful as an overcoat in a heatwave. It seemed that a dark, heavy cloud was pressing down on us. We had failed. After all the excitement of the previous few days, none of us could understand why God had done nothing for this lame boy.

The following morning I felt so low that I would not go out preaching with the team. I backed out from the session and told them to manage without me.

After they left, I tried to be pious and pray. Finally, I stopped pretending and blurted out, 'Why didn't you heal him?'

Quick as a flash, God responded, 'I have a purpose for that boy just as I have a purpose for you.' The issue was closed. God had nothing more to say on the matter.

This experience had an immediate and profound effect on me. I knew that God was dealing with me, and – in response – I hunted through my luggage for a book about the Pentecostal healing evangelist, Smith Wigglesworth, which I thought I had packed in London as medicine for just such a low moment as this. But I could not find the book anywhere. I kept on packing and unpacking the contents of my suitcase, but in vain: the book was not there. Frustrated with myself, I sat in a chair and despaired that there was nothing to restore my faith.

I was not too low to smile at myself when I finally noticed my Bible. Nothing to build my faith – how could I be so foolish? I read through the healing stories of Jesus, and it was as though I was being led by the Spirit on a personal guided tour. The Bible stories seemed amazingly real, so real that I could see myself in the situations. It was as if I was actually witnessing the events as they happened. I 'saw' Jesus touch the leper, open Bartimaeus' eye, restore Jairus' daughter, and so on. A small group of seekers huddled in a dusty field round a boy with a withered leg did not seem that far removed from the events I was reading. Suddenly the Scriptures seemed desperately relevant.

By the time I put my Bible down, I was deeply convinced of two truths. First, I realised that Jesus always ministered with an absolute certainty in the Father's willingness to heal. Of course, I knew that Jesus followed the Father's directions and healed only those to whom he was pointed: he did not pronounce blanket, indiscriminate healing to all the Judean ill. But, equally, Jesus did not need to consult with the Father when the leper asked if he was willing to heal him. Jesus did not have to stop and check whether the man was on God's list for that day, as he knew that the Father's willingness to heal extended to all.

Second, I grasped that Jesus healed everyone who came to him – humbly, simply, sometimes privately, but always all and always completely. He never said, 'Wait and see,' or 'Not today.' He never told anyone to go away and come back later.

As I sat there in a small African hut, Jesus' willingness to heal people flooded into my spirit – and has never left me since. A phrase from one of the Bible stories started running through my mind, 'Don't be afraid; only believe. Don't be afraid; only believe.' It was as though a holy tape recorder was plugged into my mind.

*E*ventually, I got up and stumbled out of the hut into the African sunlight. Where were the sick? I looked around, wondering who I was meant to heal. Just then, a messenger dashed up and started speaking rapidly in Kikuyu. A woman who was five months pregnant was miscarrying and they needed to borrow the farm van to take her to hospital. I ran across the fields to where I could see men carrying her, knowing, knowing for certain, that she would be healed.

By the time I reached the woman, I knew in my spirit what to do. I laid my hands on her, commanded healing and announced that she was healed. The farm workers ignored me and bundled her into the back of their van, which had no suspension, and they drove off down the rocky track, bouncing about in a cloud of dust.

Later, I learnt that the bleeding and pain stopped ten minutes after we had prayed, and that the men were rebuked by the hospital staff for wasting their time with a perfectly healthy woman. They fled from the hospital and, in true African fashion, immediately visited all their friends to tell them what had happened.

We had planned to show the 'Jesus' film at the farm that evening, outside in the open air. Before we began, a local evangelist arrived and asked us to go with him to a group of sick people who had gathered, five miles away, at the place where we had been expected that afternoon. (We had not been able to go because the farm van had not returned.) I told him that people were expecting to see the film, so he should bring the sick people to the farm if they wanted to be healed.

The film had already begun when this crowd arrived. We stopped the film for a moment, and I told those who wanted to be healed to come with us into the hut while the others stayed outside watching the film. Fifty people squashed into a mud hut which was lit by a flickering oil lamp. They milled around and would not get into an orderly line. I felt excited – and a little apprehensive. One particular woman kept on jostling the other people and bumping into them. I sensed myself becoming irritated with her, and hoped that I would not have to pray for her.

A young man with a paralysed arm was the first person to be prayed for. I am not sure why, but I thumped his arm – and he was instantly healed. With that, everyone in the room went quiet and still. The disorderly woman was pushed forward for prayer, and I suddenly realised why she had been bumping into people: she was completely blind. I found out later that she had walked over ten miles to the meeting, and now she just stood there grinning at me, knowing that she was going to be healed. The team grinned at me, too, but they were more nervous than confident. I laid my hands on her eyes and prayed every type of healing prayer I knew. When I took my hands away I asked her whether she could see.

She blinked and gasped, 'I can see!'

The interpreter asked her what she could see. She peered at me in the dim light, then screamed in Kikuyu: 'I can see a white man!'

There was almost a spiritual riot in the hut. Of the fifty sick people, all bar one deaf boy were completely healed in the next thirty minutes. We burst out of the door and stopped the film outside. Amazingly, they had just reached the point where Bartimaeus is healed. I gestured for silence and announced, 'While you have been watching actors acting, the real Jesus has been active in here.' The blind woman then told her story and showed them how she could see.

The people celebrated through the night. As the news spread, more and more Kenyans came running from the surrounding farms and villages. I took it in turns with the team to preach and pray for healing. When it was light, we used a nearby lake to baptise those who had given their lives to Jesus: without any suggestion from us, they all came up out of the water speaking in tongues! It was a taste of revival, the clearest that I had known at that point in my life.

Looking back, I realise that we should have changed our plans and stayed at Nyota Farm for longer, but we stuck to our itinerary and moved on to the next rural area we were scheduled to visit. Our gracious Father went on honouring our words and answering our prayers, but nothing as dramatic as the healings in the hut occurred again that trip. All too soon it was time for us to return to cynical, secular London – to comfortable homes and a large, contented church surrounded by millions of hurting people living without hope.

As we flew into Heathrow, I was determined to carry on praying for people to be healed. I promised myself that I would not go back to my old ways of ministering, for the trip had permanently freed me from the fear of experimenting and making mistakes. I was ready now to minister at home in a way which guaranteed my looking ridiculous if God did not honour my words. I told myself that, whatever the difficulties, I would stay with it until we were experiencing in London what I had tasted in that tiny African hut.

# 3

# DANCING AND
# STRUGGLING

When I was a young child, my family fled to Tanzania during the Mau Mau uprising in Kenya, and we later emigrated to Western Australia. Although my father was rather a backslidden Christian, my mother – a staunch Anglican – ensured that I was confirmed in St John's Church, Kalgoorlie, when I was ten. As a boy there, it was soon clear to everyone that I was a gifted dancer, and I came to London at sixteen to train as a professional ballet dancer.

It was in Britain, two years later in December 1971, that I was converted – through my brother's witness and the ministry of Dr Alan Redpath. This baby Christian did not know a single other believer in the whole of the city!

Soon after my conversion, I felt that I wanted to work for Christ: he had quickly become my first priority, the theatre and dance were now secondary. My guardians in England, however, would not let me give up my dance training and I submitted to their authority. I could read in the Bible, 'Submit to your elders,' so I did what the book said. I graduated into the company and danced professionally for three years, rapidly being given more important roles.

When I became a Christian, my brother told me that I needed to join a prayer group and make sure that I was baptised in water and received the Holy Spirit. So I joined a prayer group with some people from Holy Trinity, Brompton, a lively Anglican church in west London. At one of these meetings in February 1972, someone played a David Watson tape about the Holy Spirit. At the end of the tape, David Watson prayed a general prayer that I knew was for me. I asked the ascended

Christ to fill me with his Spirit, and surprised everyone in the room – including myself – by starting to pray in tongues.

I pressed the leaders of the prayer group about baptism in water, and they introduced me to a lady called Kate Waddell who attended a nearby Pentecostal church. She took me along to Kensington Temple to be baptised, and then thoroughly discipled me – and others from the ballet world who were converted at that time. For almost three years, I faithfully caught a number 28 bus every Sunday to Notting Hill Gate, never dreaming that I would still be making the same journey in twenty-five years' time. Nobody in the church could have imagined that the young ballet dancer who sometimes collected their hymn books would one day become their Senior Pastor!

After three years, a time came when I knew that I had to make a choice. For some time I had been dancing principal roles, partnering one of the company's senior ballerinas. The Director then made it clear to me that there were going to be many more roles ahead. This would have demanded such a great commitment that I would have had to forget about any ministry beyond the ballet company – and I had a deep yearning to discover and experience the sort of ministry I read about in the New Testament. Even then, I wanted to be involved in preaching *and* healing.

This time my guardians consented, and – at the age of twenty-one – I left the company to start studying for a theology diploma at Romsey House College, Cambridge. After graduating, I worked for two years with the Pye Barn Trust at a drug rehabilitation centre in south-west London. Most of my time was taken up with practical duties, but sometimes I was allowed to stand in for the Director and speak at a church meeting about the Trust's work. I longed to preach, and eagerly grasped the few opportunities for public speaking which came my way.

In the summer of 1978, I was praying in my room before one of these deputation meetings when suddenly I saw a woman in my mind. I could see exactly what she looked like, the clothes she was wearing, and where she was sitting in the church, but I did not know what to do with this visual image or how to pray about it. I guessed that God was behind the picture, but had no idea what he was suggesting to me.

When the meeting started, nobody in the church looked remotely like the woman I had imagined, and the seat she had occupied in my mind was empty. I had got it wrong again! But, just before I was due to speak, there was a kerfuffle at the door. A lady came in and sat down in the empty seat. She was almost exactly as I had imagined. The only difference was that she was blind.

I did not know what to do, so I did nothing. After the meeting I knew that I had to say something to her, so I clumsily told her that Jesus could heal her. She did not react positively to my words, and I drove home humbled and embarrassed. Things might have been different if I had had a model to follow, if I had seen Christian people acting on God's prompting, if I had had more faith and more boldness. Today I would know what to do, but then – almost twenty years ago – I failed God and I failed that lady.

After spending two demanding years at the drug centre, I served for twelve months as a church worker and very junior assistant minister at Kensington Temple before moving on to pastor a small Elim church in Bournemouth. These were dry years when I was increasingly influenced by the idea that the gifts of the Spirit had been given only to establish the Church and had ceased at the end of the New Testament era. Eventually, I stopped praying in tongues and stopped believing that contemporary miracles were real. I was spiritually ignorant and felt increasingly far from the reality and joy of the Spirit. My real joy was in my wife, Amanda, and our young daughter, Elizabeth.

During 1985, Wynne Lewis, the Senior Pastor at Kensington Temple, 'rescued' me and invited me to rejoin the staff as an assistant pastor. Through the strength of the fellowship, and the support of the other leaders, God helped me to pick up the pieces of my spiritual life. Slowly, prayer became real again and I started to review many of my foolish ideas. After a few months, however, I entered a time of deep personal testing.

I had married Amanda in 1979 – she was a senior sister in a Neonatal Special Care Unit at Queen Charlotte's Hospital in London – and our first daughter was born four years later.

18

Our second child, Laura, was born in August 1985, five months after we returned to London. She was a lovely, healthy, normal baby and we all rejoiced in the gift of a new life. Sadly, Laura developed an infection shortly after her birth and – within two days – was severely brain damaged.

Breathing difficulties quickly developed and Laura needed a machine to keep her alive. After a few more days, the doctors asked for our permission to switch the machine off. We could not agree – it seemed too much like euthanasia. Instead, this minister who had almost stopped believing in modern-day miracles cried to God to spare his daughter. Amanda and I spent two days begging our Father to intervene. At the darkest moment, we offered Laura to the Lord – and he graciously handed her back.

She began breathing on her own and started tugging at the tubes which were attached to her tiny body. Laura wasn't going to die, but she was left with severe brain damage. Scans at Great Ormond Street Hospital, the world-famous children's hospital, showed that there was hardly any brain left. All Laura's centres of speech, movement, sight and cognitive thought were destroyed. Amanda and I were told that she would live for only one year and all we could do would be to comfort her. We were devastated.

So began an intense time of learning about healing, of discovering what it means to follow the healing Christ in our hurting world. My immature understanding of healing had to move on from miracles to include wholeness. I needed to find the therapy of God's peace, and to appreciate, then appropriate, the absolute certainty of the eternal heavenly healing before us. I had to grasp – and learn how to handle – the twin realities of God's willingness to heal and the abiding presence of pain. I embraced God's living word and Laura's damaged body. I loved them both, and – through them – God taught me about his gifts of healing. Slowly, he filled my family with hope.

The Nigerian healing evangelist Benson Idahosa came to Kensington Temple that year. At first his ministry angered me. Women were yanked out of wheelchairs and their feeble on-stage hobblings were announced as holy miracles. Surely nobody could believe this was God's way and that these people were really being healed? I was not impressed. As with many 'signs and wonders' meetings I had attended, there seemed to be too much fleshly self-effort. I thought that the people were being pumped up.

After one of Benson's meetings, I spoke to an elderly lady who was tottering, stumbling, grasping chairs to stay upright. I asked her what had happened. Her eyes glistened with tears of pleasure. 'It's wonderful,' she cried, 'I haven't been able to do this for years.'

Her excited response cut through my cynicism and exposed the judgmentalism which was deep in my heart. In fact the woman lived on a further ten years and did not ever return to her wheelchair. Of course, she never walked like an athlete, but her stumblings gradually ceased. She became a symbol of hope and a visual reminder of God's grace.

I had been judging Benson's West African style of exuberant ministry and enthusiastic claims from my personal cultural viewpoint, when I should have been examining the physical improvements from the perspective of the people who were benefiting. Like most educated westerners, I had casually picked up the belief that any genuine divine healing must be instant, complete and irreversible – anything else seemed suspect. Yet I could see that my prayers for Laura's healing were being answered slowly, partially, with many setbacks. If I was eager to embrace this for myself as God's gift, I could not reject it unthinkingly for others. God was undoubtedly at work in Laura's life – and every tiny improvement boosted our hope.

Benson prayed for me at one of his final meetings, not that I would be healed but that God would use me in healing others. It was a precious and empowering experience. By this time, I knew that I would never have a ministry of my own, but I was eager to be involved in Jesus' ministry – and I realised that this should involve the sort of healing I read about in the Gospels. I was struggling, however, to find a context or framework for the miraculous which was relevant to my culture. I knew that the Holy Spirit was guiding me, but I did not know what to do with his promptings.

Through Kensington Temple – and especially the ministry of Wynne Lewis – I began to understand how God works with us. Like many people, I expected that the Spirit would somehow control me and make things happen automatically. Benson and other visiting leaders, like Charles and Paula Slagle, helped me to see that the Spirit would speak to me and that I then must act on his words. I was meant to be a partner, not a puppet.

John Wimber came to London in 1985, and I found his gentle words and ministry most helpful. He clarified the importance of hearing what the Father is saying and of then co-operating with him – of being sensitive to the Spirit and not just praying blanket prayers for everyone. Later on, Benny Hinn came too, and I found his sense of a relationship with the Spirit to be revolutionary.

These prophetic men and women opened up for me Christ's supernatural ministry. Through them I realised that everything hinged on my relationship with the Holy Spirit. I needed to live so intimately with him that I could hear his quietest promptings; I needed to submit so fully to him that I really did what he said; and I needed to depend more on his resources than on my training, experience, background and ideas.

Throughout this time of learning about healing, Amanda and I were busy caring for Laura – as well as for our elder daughter. Just before Laura's first birthday, she briefly died. We were all away at a conference when it happened. Amanda had not felt comfortable about going to one of the evening meetings and had stayed behind in our room with Laura. This meant that she was present when Laura stopped breathing. Amanda quickly checked Laura's pulse, and found that her heart was not beating either. However, with her medical expertise, Amanda was soon able to resuscitate Laura and help her through this major crisis.

Back home, we concluded that the doctors had cursed Laura when they insisted that she would live for only one year. In prayer, we broke that curse – and a time of slow recovery began. Laura's hearing and vision eventually improved to an extent which did not appear to be compatible with the Great Ormond Street scans of her brain.

We did everything we could to help her – both practically and in the realm of the Spirit. We fasted, we prayed, we anointed with oil, we removed even remotely questionable objects from our home, and so on. Finally, exhausted, we waited for God.

One day, while praying for Laura, I was suddenly overwhelmed with the Lord's presence. It was as though I was standing at the bottom of a lift shaft. Something seemed to descend and rest on my head: I knew it was an authentic experience of the exalted Christ. In my mind, I heard him speak to me and promise to lift me up and use me in a new way. Then words came which I have never forgotten. 'Do not fear, your daughter has been healed. Never doubt it.' Ten years later, even though I do not fully understand it, I am still hanging on to that prophetic message.

In 1987, about a month before I went to Kenya, I was speaking at a holiness conference for a Full Gospel Association Church in Malaysia. Half way through the week, I woke at two in the morning thinking about a certain man at the conference who was deaf in one ear and profoundly deaf in the other ear. I saw myself breaking some influence over his life and assumed that God had woken me to intercede for the man. But, somehow, I could not get hold of anything to pray.

Then the impression came to me that God was showing me what was to happen to the deaf man, but that – more importantly – he had woken me to talk about me and to deal with some deep aspects of my life. The next few hours were a time of deep forgiveness, cleansing and healing as God dealt with many attitudes and heart issues.

The Conference co-ordinator rang me first thing the following morning to say that God had shown him they must make room for 'power ministry' that day. After my own experience during the night, I agreed. I preached a message about forgiveness, then said that I wanted to pray for the delegate who was deaf in both ears. The man walked forward and, exactly as I had seen in the night vision, I first blew in the man's ear and then put my finger into his ear. He was wonderfully healed in that ear and said that he could hear the thunder rolling outside the hall. He wrote to me later to say that there had been a significant, lasting improvement in his hearing which had been medically verified.

Looking back, I can see that this moment in Malaysia was my breakthrough into supernatural ministry. Until this point, the most dramatic answer to one of my healing prayers had been in 1980, when – in response to a written prayer request about a child's broken collar bone – I had placed my hands on my own shoulder and prayed for him to be healed. While praying, I had felt a tingling sensation in my own shoulder, and the child was better within a week. It wasn't that spectacular, but it was the best that I had seen!

The joy on the Malaysian's face at hearing the thunder – and the knowledge that God had used me – gave me tremendous encouragement to press on. When I flew to Kenya a few weeks later, I was determined to be God's partner in healing. But I never imagined that he would take me so seriously and work with me so powerfully.

# 4

# NAPKIN NOTES

*O*n the plane coming home from Kenya, the four of us in the team were ecstatic. A special bond had been forged between us by the revival we had tasted together in the previous two weeks.

We knew that we were not spiritually special, and recognised that we had plenty of colleagues who were more gifted than us. When the revival took place, we assumed that the local Kenyan pastors must have been experiencing these sorts of miracles all the time. We guessed that we had unwittingly walked into their blessing and benefited from their anointing. But they all vigorously denied this when we questioned them – insisting that they had not seen anything remotely like it since T. L. and Daisy Osborne's visit many years before.

The question 'Why?' continued to grip us when we reached home. The four of us sat in a local restaurant talking about our experiences. We tried to identify the factors which had led to the 'success' and scribbled a list of ten on the back of a paper napkin. We developed these points over the next few weeks until we could not improve on them any more. Eventually, we began to absorb the ten principles into the life of the church, and these 'napkin notes' became the basis of our training programmes and ministry activity. Here they are:

1. It was God's season for a miracle. Of course, we had not been sitting about doing nothing waiting for God to work. We had prayed and been willing to co-operate with him. But, ultimately, there had not been anything we could do to guarantee that healing miracles would occur. If it had not been God's time for miracles at Nyota Farm, none of them would have occurred.

2. We went apostolically. We knew that 'being sent' was the essence of apostleship, and we had not turned up in Kenya as spiritual tourists and imposed our presence. The initiative came from the local African leaders and we were sent there by the elders at our church in London. Kensington Temple had not sent only money and books – useful though these are – they had also sent us and we had willingly gone. We were sure from our reading of the New Testament that our active, personal 'going' with the gospel was an important factor in the blessing.

3. We went with humility and a servant's attitude. Our trip had involved an element of hardship and sacrifice. We slept and ate with the people, shared their simple homes, used their primitive facilities, and expected no payment for our time and services. We went knowing that we would learn more than we taught and receive more than we gave.

4. We concentrated on ministering to ordinary working people – to those with considerable needs who knew they were needy. We had not gone to the educated, the affluent, the powerful or those who could repay us, but to those whom we believed the New Testament suggests are highest on God's agenda.

5. The four of us functioned in unity as a team. We knew that Jesus sent out the twelve apostles and the seventy disciples to preach and heal in pairs, so I had not gone on my own. Although I was the leader and principal speaker, the others were deeply involved in every aspect of the ministry.

6. We carefully prepared ourselves beforehand with much prayer, fasting and intercession for the ministry, our safety and our families while we were away. Many people in our church prayed for us diligently throughout the trip.

7. We preached an uncompromising gospel which embraced both healing and forgiveness. We were convinced that as followers of the living Jesus, we were supposed to announce all the good news of God's kingdom. So we urged our African listeners to repent, to believe in Jesus, to accept God's forgiveness, to show that they were turning to God by being baptised and receiving the Spirit, and to commit themselves whole-heartedly to a life of disciplined obedience to God's personal rule. We also made it pretty clear that God wanted to heal

every aspect of their lives, emotions and bodies, and offered to pray for those who wanted to experience some form of healing. We did not merely pray for the people *en masse*, but also personally and individually.

8. On the trip, we concentrated particularly intently on living with careful holiness. We were separated to the task and continually encouraged each other to think and to act and to treat people in a thoroughly Christ-like way.

9. Being away from Britain meant that we were free from emotional, cultural, intellectual and ecclesiastical restraints. We all felt able to take risks and generally 'go for it'.

10. We operated 'in faith' and under a general atmosphere of faith – or belief. We depended on what we understood to be God's promptings, using the gifts of God's Spirit as they were given to us, and the people we were ministering to genuinely believed that they were going to be healed – they really trusted us!

We had thought that all our friends in London would be as thrilled as we were with our news, but most people could not relate to our stories of blind eyes opening and deaf ears hearing. 'Ah well,' they said, 'that's Africa. It won't happen here.'

Many people looked at us blankly when we described what had happened. Some asked why we could not do the same things here. Others accused us of boasting or exaggerating. This hurt. I did not want to take any credit for our experiences, but I knew that I had played my part as one of God's partners.

As a team, we had been convinced that God would repeat the miracles when we started preaching again in London. But he didn't – at least, not to the same degree. When we got over our initial disappointment at the obvious change of spiritual season, I recalled a remark that I had made at the height of the miracles in Nyota Farm. I remembered enthusing to my colleagues, 'Heaven is wide open to us. This is like being in London ten years from now!' There had been no apparent basis for these words and, repeatedly reflecting on them, I gradually came to believe that I had spoken a serious and profound prophecy.

Those three weeks in Africa were undoubtedly my most

important formative experience in ministry. Since then, I have found it hard to settle for anything less. Through the events I tasted in Kenya, a radical pentecostalism began to be birthed in me which has gone on to shape and direct my thinking, my actions and my share in the ministry of Christ.

Wynne Lewis, the Senior Pastor at Kensington Temple, was wonderfully supportive and enthusiastic on our return. He helped me start to apply in the church what I had learnt in Africa, and encouraged me to travel and learn some more. I determined on four core values that I wanted to build at the centre of our church life. These were:

1. personal and corporate discipleship
2. world vision
3. signs and wonders
4. a passion for evangelism.

Together, we tried to create a wide variety of learning experiences for as many of our members as possible so that these four core values could be established and grow. We developed seminars and courses on which people could learn to minister. We set up many more overseas mission trips, created healing teams to serve in our meetings and out on the streets, and focused on planting new churches across London so that large numbers of people could be released in ministry.

In 1991, Wynne was appointed General Superintendent of the British Elim Pentecostal Churches, and the elders at Kensington Temple invited me to take over as Senior Pastor. With this move, radical pentecostalism began to assume an even higher profile in my life and the church's activities. At first, I felt exposed and vulnerable as leader. Laura was six years old by then and I was often tempted to feel that her condition disqualified me from being a credible witness to God's healing power.

The long struggle of learning to cope with Laura's condition has been a real test, but I now know that my faith and courage have been considerably increased by dealing with her difficulties. Amanda, however, often has a terrible time when I am away: it is as though, when God works through me in a special way, the enemy retaliates by lashing at my most precious and vulnerable point.

The issue of Laura's healing is never in my mind when I am praying with people for them to receive God's healing. I do not doubt that God's promise to me for her healing will be fulfilled, and I long for the day when this releases Amanda from the endless round of care. A few years ago, in Africa, I saw a young boy partially healed from cerebral palsy: his neck muscles were miraculously strengthened and he was suddenly able to make eye contact with the people around him. An incident like this fills me with hope for Laura. None of us needs everyone to be healed and restored in order to receive hope for a loved one – just one genuine healing provides hope for all.

Through all the difficulties, God has used Laura to increase my compassion and sense of impotence. Some leaders say that they easily become numb to the pain of the people they are helping. They are so busy ministering that they stop being moved by the procession of broken lives and the sea of distressed faces. It is no credit to me that I respond differently. God has filled me with so much compassion for Laura that it naturally overflows to others who are facing hardship and pain.

Equally, a few leaders are so 'professional' in the way they minister, they give the impression that they can deal with any problem. In an attempt to build people's faith, they focus too much attention on themselves and seem to suggest that they themselves can do anything. But I know that I follow one who constantly emphasised the fact that – of himself – he could say and do nothing, and daily involvement with Laura has driven this truth deep into my conscious thought and experience. I have no delusions: I know that, by myself, I am fundamentally impotent.

Of course, as God, Jesus was able to cast out demons, heal the sick, raise the dead, walk on water, feed thousands from a lunchbox and turn water into gallons of wine. But he had chosen not to 'use' his divinity, and he also made it clear that – in his humanity – he was utterly powerless. The miraculous did not occur because Jesus was God, but because he was filled with the Spirit without measure and always moved in perfect harmony with the Father. As a result of my involvement with Laura, whenever God speaks or acts through me today, I know that it really is all his work. I might be his partner, but he contributes all the power.

1 have been the Senior Pastor at Kensington Temple since 1991, and in that time we have developed a much broader sense of healing. We have started to appreciate the extent to which God wants to make us all fully whole: this process includes miraculous signs and wonders, but God wants to go beyond the purely physical to heal us emotionally, psychologically, intellectually, socially and spiritually.

Restored marriages, reunited families, days free from depression and stress, healthy lifestyles, good nutrition, an attitude that looks to eternity and sees death as the gateway to fuller life – these are as much a part of the wholeness God wants to bring to our lives as instant, physical healings of sickness and disability. Our Father wants us to apply his gospel at every level of human living and to become like Jesus in every aspect of our lives.

Although most British people yearn for some sort of life-transforming miracle – which is why they play the national lottery – many of them are uncomfortable with the idea of physical healing miracles. This means that there is often a pressure on church leaders to define healing in a wider, less physical, way. Nearly all Christian believers must be familiar with every possible reason why healing miracles cannot, should not and do not happen today! Some Christians have reacted to this by over-emphasising the miraculous or by making unhelpful claims. My experience suggests that the whole area of healing is a tapestry which should be woven with different threads, and the full picture is both weakened and diminished when we ignore or overstate any one aspect.

A lady had been injured in an industrial accident when she was nineteen. For the following sixteen years she experienced such severe pain from a chronic inflammatory condition that she had to wear splints on both arms, was frequently bedridden, and often needed to use a wheelchair. She could walk around the home using furniture for support, but needed a wheelchair when she went out.

She had spent many long years waiting for healing, clinging

to scriptural promises yet often feeling terribly depressed. She was sure that God was going to heal her some day, that he had told her through a dream he would restore her, but she did not know when this would be.

A few years ago, she attended a Bible Week in her usual wheelchair. I was speaking at the last meeting when I sensed that God was going to heal a nurse who had been injured in an industrial accident. When I announced this, she was convinced that God was speaking directly to her and knew that he wanted to do something important in her life. During a time of general ministry after the sermon, she believed that she should walk forward to the front where people had gathered for prayer. She got out of her wheelchair and struggled slowly forward – every step was agony.

When she eventually reached the front, she wanted to raise an arm in the air like the other people praying. She had not been able to do this for over ten years, but suddenly found that she could. Next she was able to raise her other arm, and then she felt God's power in every joint in turn in her body. There at the front of the meeting, she managed to move her body in ways which had not been possible for years.

She visited her doctor as soon as she returned home, and he was amazed to see her walking, without any splints on her arms, without a chair or stick as support. He did not know what to make of her extraordinary improvement.

Her husband and twelve-year-old daughter did not know what to do either, for they had known her only as immobile. They had never seen her active, and expected her to remain in a chair while they did everything for her. But now she could walk eight miles without discomfort, go on holiday, do the shopping and housework – and the whole family struggled with the shock of the miracle. Her child was even reluctant to go to school.

God's whole healing for this family continued long after the original physical improvement as – with his help – they adjusted to a new way of living together. True wholeness would not have been possible without the physical change, but the miracle needed to go much further than that.

$\mathcal{A}$s we have tried at Kensington Temple to build upon our 'napkin notes', so we have – perhaps inevitably – experienced some sort of tension between our emphasis on healing others as part of 'going out with the gospel' and our experience of receiving healing 'here at the meetings'. Most people seem to feel comfortable with an organised time of prayer for healing at the end of services, they can handle that without too much embarrassment. But they are less keen on healing at other times and places – especially when they are the person who has to do all the praying!

Bishop David Pytches has coined this helpful phrase, 'the meeting place is the learning place for the market place'. If Christ and his cross are central to our meetings, we can surely expect him to express every aspect of his ministry in our regular services. When people come hoping to meet with the risen Christ in all his resurrection power, I can hardly tell them that there is no room in the meeting for his healing power and the healing of the cross. We must, however, also continually teach, train, encourage and urge our members to demonstrate the power of Christ wherever they are during the week.

It is hard always to get the balance right, but many things have happened which have greatly encouraged me. After one of our meetings, a seventeen-year-old boy was returning home on the Underground when he noticed a woman carrying a child with leg-irons. He asked the mother if he could pray for her son as he believed that Jesus wanted to heal him. She said that he could pray for the child, but only when he got to his home. She did not want a scene in the Tube. The young man agreed and gave her the church's telephone number, asking her to make contact if the boy was healed.

He did pray fervently for the boy when he arrived at his home. And the woman did notice something different about her child when she reached her home. She took his leg-irons off and found that he was 'completely healed'. So she rang the church to find out what she should do next!

Because Christian people do need to meet together regularly for worship, prayer and teaching, most church meetings are rightly aimed at believers. But the tendency to offer healing mainly at such meetings can lead some people to think of

31

healing primarily as a pastoral activity. There is an important place for pastoral healing, but too great a stress on it can cause us to forget that healing is essentially a sign pointing unbelievers to God. Therefore, as well as encouraging people in mission and establishing healing teams which go out into the community, we keep on trying to create evangelistic contexts where we can pray for sick unbelievers.

In every church there are bound to be constant challenges to faith. There are usually a few members who are chronically and critically ill, and the challenge of helping them should be used to prepare us for reaching out more widely with God's healing. All pastors bury people whom they have prayed for, and we will not fully understand or experience God's wholeness if we exclude death from our theology of healing. We must resist, however, the temptation to downplay God's willingness to heal people physically and the widespread availability of his resurrection power.

Kensington Temple is a church with, in 1997, over 6,000 people in fellowship and a further 6,000 in its satellite network. This means that we have had our share of tests and tragedies in the past few years – as well as an increasing number of wonderful miracles!

Three years ago, one of our young members went into hospital to have her tonsils removed. She was a second-year medical student and was being treated at the London hospital where she was studying. Tragically, she suffered an allergic reaction to the anaesthetic drugs. Her brain was starved of oxygen for five minutes, and she had to be placed on a life support machine.

We mobilised the church to pray, and it seemed sensible to ask the Lord to take her to be with him. Common sense said that she would not be healed as nerve cells in the brain die when the oxygen supply is interrupted for as little as two or three minutes. Yet, somehow, I just could not bring myself to ask people to pray for her to die – so together we asked God to heal her.

She was in a deep coma for almost three weeks and suffered many serious complications: her EEG was grossly abnormal, her scans showed severe cerebral oedema, her infusion site was infected with the dreaded MRSA, and she had developed involuntary movements and spasticity of her limbs and body. On the Coma Scale, which ranges from 15, consciousness, to a minimum of 3, deep coma, she fluctuated between 3 and 6. Throughout this grim time, the church united in praying for God to heal her.

Seventeen days after the allergic reaction, the consultant announced that she would remain in a permanent vegetative state. The same day, she opened her eyes and identified several members of her family. The medical staff then promised that she would never walk or see properly; but she was walking with support after six weeks, was starting to see after three months, and – two and a half years later – is about to return to her medical training.

It is wonderful how an incident like this affects the whole church and brings hope to large numbers of people who are struggling with a problem which needs divine healing. Even the best we offer of the biblical teaching about wholeness never galvanises people into hope and expectancy like a single genuine miracle.

Someone may list all the scriptural examples of healing, may understand how God works through the cross and the Spirit, may appreciate the way that God acts through anointed believers – and still find it difficult to pray with faith for themselves or a sick friend. Yet faith wells up without any effort when that person sees or hears about God's healing power.

If we prayed for, say, fifty sick people and forty-nine remained ill, secular cynics and sceptical Christians would focus on the forty-nine and ignore the one miracle – or try to explain it away. Genuine believers would not ignore those who seemed to be unchanged, or try to blame them for some supposed lack of faith, or explain them away in embarrassment. Rather, they would help and support them, and rejoice with them about the one who was healed; and they would allow this experience permanently to affect the way that they thought and believed.

Ten years on from my first trip to Kenya, I have now seen much which has exceeded that precious experience of God's power. It was my first major experience of authentic, miraculous healings and it continues to encourage me to go on seeking, asking and believing for signs and wonders. My day-to-day experience of Laura's condition does not negate incidents like Nyota Farm; instead, it ensures that my thinking about healing is tempered by the dynamic tensions and struggles of our hurt and broken world.

This book is a sort of healing journey – rooted in pain and the miraculous – towards godly hope. In the next section I set out what I see God's word teaching about miraculous healing; then I grapple with some of the issues which concern people in western nations; and finally, I offer a framework for contemporary Christian healing – and some enthusiastic encouragement for you to take the plunge.

I have not written this book so that you can learn about *my* share in Christ's ministry, I have written it so that *you* will start partnering God, *you* will begin taking God's hope to the people around you, *you* will make God's healing voice heard, and *you* will join me in praying that God will grant a season of supernatural blessing – in your own nation, in your own day.

# Part Two

# LOOKING AT THE SCRIPTURES

# 5

# THE PROPHETS' ANOINTING

W hen I read the Scriptures, it is plain to me that they reveal our God as being deeply involved with the healing and wholeness of all his children. The Old Testament presents Yahweh Rapha, the living God of Israel, as a God who is concerned about the basic hygiene and nutrition of his people, who binds up their broken hearts, who comforts and counsels them, and who heals them of their diseases.

I see that the Old Testament is packed with promises of healing: Exodus 15:26; Deuteronomy 32:39; Psalm 103:3; Proverbs 3:7–8; Ecclesiastes 3:3; Isaiah 19:22, 30:26, 57:18–19; Jeremiah 30:17; Hosea 6:1; Malachi 4:2. It records prayers for healing: 1 Samuel 1:10–11; Psalm 6:2, 41:4; Jeremiah 17:14. It offers joyful testimonies of healing: 1 Samuel 1:19–2:11; Psalm 30:2, 107:20, 147:3. And it honestly describes concern about a lack of healing: Jeremiah 15:18. In particular, the Old Testament describes nine incidents which help us start to understand how God intervenes in the lives of his children to bring about a wonderful healing.

I doubt whether the healing miracles recorded in the Bible are the totality of miracles which occurred in those days, just as the stories I have included in this book are only a tiny selection from my experience. Instead, I suspect that the scriptural examples have been preserved for us in the word by the Spirit because they illustrate important principles about the way that the Father heals.

In this and the next two chapters, we will look at those healing miracles which are reported in the Bible, and will try to identify some basic divine healing principles. Then, in

37

chapter eight, we will examine the contexts which seem to be fundamental to the New Testament healing miracles. After that, we will think about some of the wider issues arising from the biblical teaching about healing and health, and will try to establish a balance which can keep us from slipping into an unhelpful extremism.

The first scriptural healing incident, in Genesis 20, describes the cure of Abimelech and all the women of his household from impotence and barrenness. As the first specific example of a healing miracle, it lays down many principles which are repeated throughout the Bible. Abraham was God's partner in this healing, and – in verse 7 – he is identified by God as a prophet.

This is the first time that the Bible mentions a prophet, and the events of Genesis 20 establish the scriptural link between prophetic activity, intercession and miraculous healing. This link runs on throughout the Bible and church history to today. I cannot overstate how important it is that we grasp this link – it is fundamental to the Church's healing ministry.

Prophets were the intercessors, healers and miracle-workers of the Old Testament. Only they – by virtue of their special anointing with God's Spirit – had the right of access to God's face which was essential for these activities. It seems to me that contemporary Christian leaders and believers drift into a variety of well-meaning but mistaken ideas when they miss the critical relationship between prophetic anointing and prophetic activity: between an anointing with the Spirit and interceding with God, hearing God's thoughts and powerfully passing on his words and his healing.

As well as recognising Abraham's prophetic anointing, it is also important for us to appreciate his sinfulness. God answered Abraham's prayers and used him in healing even though he had been attempting to deceive Abimelech out of fear for his own life. I find this foundation healing miracle so encouraging because it shows that our gracious God does not demand perfect partners but works with and through flawed, fearful people who love and serve him.

I think that we must also appreciate the significance of

Abimelech and his household to the story. The first person in the Scriptures to benefit from a healing miracle was not one of God's favourite children, it was a pagan king – one of the first rulers of the Philistines, who came to symbolise the enemies of God's people. This story establishes that healing is part of the interaction between God's anointed servants and people who do not serve and follow God. We could say that this miracle is set in an essentially evangelistic context.

Genesis 20 also suggests the idea that sickness may be allowed by God as some sort of curse or punishment, but that – through prophetic intercession – God will revoke his action. (We will consider this idea in more detail in chapter eleven.) For Abimelech, the healing would be a sign pointing to the more important fact that he was forgiven by God.

We cannot know the time scale involved in this healing, but several months must have passed before Abimelech had convincing proof that all the members of his household had been cured. The actual miracle could have been instant and complete, but Abimelech's appreciation of the healing must have been gradual.

It is also instructive that the first biblical report of miraculous healing involves the person who is consistently identified by the Scriptures as the great symbol of saving faith. Most evangelical and pentecostal believers are used to referring to Abraham when they think about the place of faith in salvation. Genesis 20 shows that we should also remember his faith when we think about healing.

According to the Scriptures, Abraham received by faith the covenant from God about a year before his encounter with Abimelech. We should note that when God gave Abraham the covenant, he also gave him a sign to confirm his word – the promise of a child, which would involve the healing of Sarah's infertility. This suggests three ideas: first, that the Bible lays down a link between salvation and healing; second, that healing miracles are divine signs given to reassure and encourage us that God's word is true and reliable; and, third, that God is concerned for his covenant people to receive healing from him.

This sign, however, did not materialise immediately. Sarah

was still not pregnant a year later when she met Abimelech – but this did not prevent Abraham from faithfully praying to God for Abimelech's household to be healed of infertility. I have found that God often calls his partners to pray for a particular type of healing in others which they yearn for themselves but have not experienced, even though God may have clearly promised to bring the healing about. It is interesting to see that the Scriptures record that Sarah became pregnant immediately after the members of Abimelech's household were healed by God through Abraham's prophetic prayers. This encourages me so much in my hopes and prayers for Laura.

The second scriptural healing incident, recorded in Numbers 12, tells the story of Miriam's healing from leprosy. This story repeats some of the ideas seen in the first story: a prophet – Moses – was God's partner in healing; Miriam's sickness was a punishment sent by God; the healing was a sign pointing to her forgiveness; the miracle was not revealed instantly to anybody. In this case, however, the person healed was one of God's leading servants and we can say that the miracle clearly is set in a pastoral context.

Numbers 12 introduces an element which features in several scriptural stories and still seems important today. The person who wants to be healed is given an action to perform which facilitates the healing – here, for example, Miriam had to remain outside the camp for seven days. In my experience, people who want to be healed by God are often required by him to identify themselves in some way, perhaps by responding to a prophetic message, or to evidence their faith in his ability to heal them.

The third incident, in 1 Kings 13, shows both that there can be a place for fasting in healing and that God's partner must always obey God's orders unconditionally. A prophet, who was under a divine order to fast, denounced the altar that King Jeroboam had made for a golden calf. Jeroboam angrily ordered that the prophet be seized, but God instantly withered the king's hand. Jeroboam knew that only a prophet could placate God and bring healing, and urged the prophet to pray for him. The prophet interceded with God and the king's hand was healed –

again, the miracle was a sign pointing to the more important reality of God's forgiveness.

Yet, within hours, God's healing partner lay dead, mauled by a lion. Why? Simply because the prophet had been deceived into disobeying God's personal instruction to fast. Although it is extremely rare for God to punish disobedience in this way, the story does show how seriously God takes his healing instructions. I do not think it is very likely that we will be mauled by a lion today if we are tricked into disobeying God, but we must never think that we can treat God's prophetic promptings lightly.

In 1 Kings 17:8–24, we read the story of Elijah's stay with a widow at Zarephath. When the widow's son died, she blamed Elijah. She did not understand the goodness of God and assumed that the presence of a prophet had revealed her secret or unconscious sins and drawn divine retribution. Elijah took the boy's body, carried it to his bed, then cried out to God in intercession. As far as we know, Elijah had no precedents for his prayers for resuscitation, but that did not stop him praying. None of us would ever pray for healing if we restricted our praying to those particular miracles that we had already seen God perform! God soon answered the prophet's persistent prayers and Elijah gave the revived boy back to his mother.

We know that Elisha inherited a double portion of Elijah's prophetic anointing, so it is instructive to note that more Old Testament healing miracles are associated with Elisha than with anyone else, and that most of the people healed were pagans. This seems to underscore the biblical link between the Spirit's anointing, miraculous healing and evangelism.

Two episodes are related in 2 Kings 4:8–37 involving Elisha and a Shunammitess. A notable woman in Shunem was hospitable to Elisha and his servant Gehazi, and this prompted Elisha to offer to speak to the king on her behalf. She did not want a material reward, so Elisha prophetically announced that she would give birth to a son in twelve months' time.

As we have seen with Sarah, Abraham and Abimelech, and as with many other scriptural examples of healing, there must have been a delayed appreciation of this miracle. It is obvious that the woman would not have had evidence of conception

41

for many months, or of the child's sex until it was born! Many people assume that there must be some immediate, tangible evidence if a miracle is instantaneous. Yet this is not always what the Scriptures describe. Time and again, there is a gap in the Bible stories between God's word and what we would consider to be convincing proof of a miracle; and God still sometimes calls us to live with patient faith in that gap between his word and our personal experience.

When we think about it dispassionately, there are bound to be many such instances. God rarely deals in fantasy miracles whereby an infertile woman is told that she will give birth in five seconds' time! He normally works through the natural processes he designed – and they take rather longer.

We have seen that many of the biblical healing miracles involve the healing of childlessness – and there are stories of other people, like Hannah and Elizabeth, where God opened a closed womb to bring a mighty prophet into being. I have found that this emphasis on healing infertility is repeated today at our church. Two years ago one of our members was holding a service at a hospital chapel and praying for people's needs when a man walked in and requested prayer as he had just learnt that he and his wife could not conceive. Only a few minutes earlier, a consultant had told him that his sperm count was only 2 per cent of normal and that his wife had fibroids and blocked fallopian tubes.

The member prayed with the man in the chapel, and later at length with the couple in their home. After much prayer, the member felt led prophetically to announce that the couple would conceive within three months. The woman then had to enter hospital for an operation to remove her fibroids, but the surgeon found that her fallopian tubes were no longer blocked and that the fibroids had disappeared. Ten weeks after the prophetic announcement, the couple rang the member to announce that they were expecting a baby without any medical treatment!

In 2 Kings 4, the barren Shunammitess gave birth to a boy, who developed normally and then died unexpectedly. But her faith in Elisha remained absolute – he had obtained a son for her, therefore he could restore him – and she set off to see

Elisha. The prophet gave Gehazi his staff – a symbol of his prophetic authority – and sent him to stretch it over the corpse. Nothing happened. So Elisha came himself, went into the bedroom alone with the body, and started to pray. In this example, the healing partner was given an unusual task to aid the healing process. Elisha climbed on to the body and lay on it. When the flesh felt warm, he stepped off. Elisha repeated this seven times before the dead boy sneezed and revived.

The healing of Naaman, in 2 Kings 5, was another cure which was initiated by a human request, and in which there is no hint that the sickness was due to personal sin. The Aramaean army commander drew up in his chariot at Elisha's house. Instead of speaking to him in person, the prophet sent a messenger with the details of a God-given task which Naaman had to fulfil to facilitate the healing. Naaman's indignation, in verse 11, has a contemporary ring to it: 'Indeed, I said to myself, "He will surely come out to me, and stand and call on the name of the Lord his God, and wave his hand over the place, and heal the leprosy."' Naaman needed to learn the lessons we still need to learn today, that healing is a matter of obedience not technique, and that it is due to divine intervention not human perspiration. Eventually, Naaman's pride was punctured by his servants' words and he obediently immersed himself seven times in the river Jordan.

As a result of the healing, Naaman recognised that Yahweh alone was truly God and pressed Elisha to accept a gift. He refused. He knew that God's partners should take no credit or reward for something that God alone has done. So, instead of thanking man, Naaman praised God and loaded a pair of mules with soil from Israel on which to build an altar to Yahweh in Damascus. He rode off in his chariot, healed and blessed, the first scriptural example of a convert through a healing miracle. We read in Luke 4:27 that Jesus was to look back to this evangelistic story and claim it as a precedent for his entire ministry.

Naaman is the forerunner of all the people today who turn to God because of their experience of healing. His condition was obviously unpleasant, but – unlike most lepers – it was not severe enough to cause social isolation and unemployment.

Even so, God reached out and healed Naaman as he obediently responded to God's words through the anointed prophet.

The fourth healing story involving Elisha is rather unusual: 2 Kings 13:20–21 records another wonderful resuscitation, yet is rarely referred to today. Out of fear of raiding Moabites, some Israelites tossed a dead friend into Elisha's tomb. Apparently, the body bounced against the bones of the dead prophet and sprang to life!

In this incident, there appears to have been no faith and no intercession – only fear and panic. We do not know how long Elisha had been dead, and some wonder about a residual effect of his double anointing. All we can say for certain is that God is not tame or predictable. We cannot imprison him in our healing techniques and traditions. I have often had to be reminded that the living God works miracles how, when, and through whom he wills – and sometimes it is through individuals and in ways which many of us find culturally inappropriate, theologically uncomfortable and terribly embarrassing.

We should not pretend that this particular incident is absent from the Bible, but neither should we return to the Church's practice in the Middle Ages of venerating the bones of deceased prophets and urging sick people to touch them. Equally, we should not automatically dismiss the documented cases in medieval church history when it is claimed that God used a similar means in healing. The Elisha story should teach us cultural humility and spiritual openness. It teaches us nothing about healing techniques, it is merely a sign or pointer to God's unlimited grace and power.

The final healing miracle to be mentioned in the Old Testament, in 2 Kings 20:1–11, describes the cure of King Hezekiah's ulcer or boil. The prophet Isaiah was sent by God to announce the king's imminent death. Hezekiah wept and pleaded with God – and God changed his mind. So Isaiah was sent back to announce three things: a healing which would take place in the near future; a fifteen-year life expectancy; and the immediate prospect of peace for Jerusalem. In this case, God's partner was given a task to carry out: Isaiah summoned a servant, ordered a fig poultice, applied it to the ulcer, and the king recovered. It is unlikely that there was immediate evidence of the cure, for the king asked for proof that he would survive the next three days, a proof which God graciously supplied through his anointed prophet.

These Old Testament examples emphasise the sovereignty and power of God. They do not teach us much about how God's covenant people personally receive healing for themselves from Yahweh Rapha. Some important healing principles emerge from them, however, in relation to the part we must play as God's partners in healing others, and these we would do well to appreciate.

1. The ministry of healing was an activity which was exclusive to God's servants the prophets – God worked in partnership *only* with and through those whom he had anointed with his Spirit as prophets.

2. The sickness was occasionally due to personal sin.

3. In some cases, either God's partner or the sick person needed to perform an action as part of the healing ministry.

4. The prophetic partner either interceded with God for the healing or announced its arrival.

5. Prophets did not go around offering healing. They responded to human requests and to God's prompting through the Spirit.

6. The people healed were not necessarily Jews – more than half of the people healed were outside the covenant. Overall, there was a balance between what we can call 'pastoral' and 'evangelistic' healings.

7. Some element of faith or expectancy was normally present.

8. Many of the healings would not have appeared to be instant – there was often a delayed appreciation of the healing.

9. Most of the healings were signs which directed the person's attention to something far more significant – often to the gift of forgiveness.

10. Sometimes none of these Old Testament principles applied and God intervened in a sovereign and mysterious way.

We should not think that all the Old Testament prophets were involved with physical healing for clearly many of them were not. We can say, however, that all the people who ministered God's healing were anointed prophets.

Equally, we should not think that healing was the primary calling of any prophet as it is plain that reconciliation with the living God of Israel dominated the prophets' ministries. Healing was, however, a natural part of the proclamatory and intercessory sides of their work.

The prophets constantly reminded people of what God had done – at times they almost functioned as court historians – and they used the past to reveal God's nature and to proclaim what God was about to do. They knew that God always acts consistently with his nature.

The events of the Exodus dominated Israel's understanding of God and, as we have seen, this was founded on God's revelation of himself as Yahweh Rapha, the Lord who heals. So when the prophets called people to return to the God of Moses, to the God who had been with them in the wilderness, to the God who had divided the Red Sea, they were essentially pointing people to the healing God. If we do not grasp this, our understanding of healing will not be founded in God, and our understanding of God will be incomplete. Like the Old Testament prophets, we can trust God – we can expect God – always to act consistently with his self-revealed nature. He is the reliable healer.

# 6

# ANOINTED WITHOUT MEASURE

At the time of Christ, there was a widespread Jewish expectation that when the long-expected Messiah finally arrived he would be another prophet, one who would fulfil Moses' prophecy in Deuteronomy 18:15–20. Throughout his ministry, Jesus was recognised as a prophet by his friends and enemies because of what he said and did. In Acts 3:22–24, for example, Peter showed that he believed Jesus to be 'the prophet'. Jesus was the supreme prophet, mighty in word and deed, who was anointed with the Spirit without measure.

Some people today believe that Jesus healed the sick only because he was divine. But such was the Jewish understanding of the scriptural link between the miraculous and the Spirit's anointing, that the response of those who observed his miracles was to identify him as a prophet – not to name him as God. They knew that the only people who healed and worked miracles were prophets. In John 9:17, the Pharisees asked the beggar what he had to say about Jesus now that Jesus had opened his eyes. He replied, 'He is a prophet.' John 6:14 makes it clear that the people fed by the loaves and fishes leapt to the same conclusion.

Jesus always was the perfect Son of God, but few people suspected his divine origin or prophetic office until after his public anointing with the Spirit at his baptism by John in the River Jordan. This was the moment when the Father anointed Jesus with the Spirit to commission him as Messiah and to equip him for his messianic task.

Jesus left the river filled with the Spirit; he was driven into the desert by the Spirit; he overcame satanic temptation; and

– full of the power of the Spirit – he returned to Galilee ~~re~~, in his home synagogue, he introduced himself as the ~~fu~~ ilment of Isaiah 61:1–2. Luke 4:16–30 describes how the local carpenter sensationally proclaimed that, because he had been anointed with the Spirit, he was now healing the broken-hearted, liberating the oppressed and giving new sight to the blind.

In the Nazareth synagogue Jesus boldly identified himself as a prophet and clearly linked himself with Elijah's healing miracle at Zarephath and Elisha's evangelistic healing encounter with Naaman. Jesus was claiming to be another healing prophet, like Elijah and Elisha, whose healing ministry, like theirs, would be mainly to those outside the kingdom – with the aim of drawing them, like Naaman, into the kingdom of God.

If we think that Jesus healed people only because he was divine, it is likely we will assume that we can have no share in his healing ministry. Whereas, if we grasp that he healed because he was anointed, we can reasonably expect to have some part in his healing ministry – as long as we are anointed with the same Spirit. However, Jesus' divinity, sinlessness, perfect obedience and unlimited anointing must surely mean that we cannot always expect to be as effective in ministry as him.

The four Gospels accredit about twenty specific healing incidents to Jesus – not including those occasions when he cast out demons: (1) the nobleman's son at Capernaum: John 4:43–54; (2) Jairus' daughter: Matthew 9:18–26; Mark 5:22–43; Luke 8:41–56; (3) the woman with the issue of blood: Matthew 9:20–22; Mark 5:25–34; Luke 8:43–48; (4) two blind men: Matthew 9:27–31; (5) the paralysed man let down through the roof: Matthew 9:1–8; Mark 2:2–12; Luke 5:17–26; (6) a leper: Matthew 8:1–4; Mark 1:40–45; Luke 5:12–14; (7) the centurion's servant: Matthew 8:5–13; Luke 7:1–10; (8) Peter's mother-in-law: Matthew 8:14–15; Mark 1:29–31; Luke 4:38–39; (9) the widow of Nain's son: Luke 7:11–17; (10) the lame man at the pool of Bethesda: John 5:1–15; (11) the man born blind: John 9:1–41; (12) the man with the withered hand:

Matthew 12:9–14; Mark 3:1–6; Luke 6:6–11; (13) the woman bent double: Luke 13:10–17; (14) the man with dropsy: Luke 14:1–6; (15) the ten lepers: Luke 17:11–19; (16) the deaf and dumb man: Mark 7:31–37; (17) the blind man of Bethsaida: Mark 8:22–26; (18) Lazarus: John 11:1–44; (19) the blind men of Jericho: Matthew 20:29–34; Mark 10:46–52; Luke 18:35–43; and (20) the high priest's servant: Luke 22:49–51.

The Gospels also record about twelve general statements about Jesus' healing activity. These are reported in (1) Matthew 4:23–25; Luke 6:17–19; (2) Matthew 8:16–17; Mark 1:32–34; Luke 4:40; (3) Matthew 11:4–5; Luke 7:21–22; (4) Matthew 9:35; (5) Matthew 12:15–16; Mark 3:10–12; (6) Matthew 14:14; Luke 9:11; John 6:2; (7) Matthew 14:34–36; Mark 6:54–56; (8) Matthew 15:30–31; (9) Matthew 19:2; (10) Matthew 21:14; (11) Luke 5:15; and (12) Luke 8:1–2.

From these passages, we can begin to develop some durable New Testament principles about divine healing which are relevant for Christ's body, the Church, today. The twenty healing incidents introduce us to around thirty people who were cured by God through Jesus: twenty-four men, three women, three children and a servant whose sex is not specified. Obviously many more people were healed, but these thirty seem to have been singled out by the Spirit as special examples for us to learn from.

The Old Testament prophets are reported as often being involved with healing people in authority – kings, an army commander, a women of rank, a high priest's sister – whereas the Gospels describe Jesus focusing on social outcasts. Nineteen of the thirty examples of healing were people at the edge of society, and most of the rest were common people suffering from terrible afflictions.

I am convinced that we need to share Jesus' 'heart' if we are to share in his ministry. He came to find the lost, to release the prisoners and to heal the broken-hearted. This surely means that we should be eager to minister to the marginalised groups of people who live at the edge of contemporary society – prisoners and their families, refugees, the mentally ill. Of course, God is also very willing to heal more well-to-do believers, but we need to ensure that his healing gospel is felt more widely, especially among the alienated and the poor.

Visitors to Kensington Temple are often struck by the multiracial make-up of our congregation. Many of our members are drawn from Black and Asian ethnic groups, and some are from the poorer social groups in London. Opponents of the healing ministry often comment disparagingly on the credibility of healing testimonies from less well-educated believers. They suggest that the uneducated are gullible and that their testimony cannot be relied upon. In Chapter 12 we will look at the important issues of medical verification and the definition of miracles, but we ought to be able to agree that people do not have to be university graduates to grasp that a pain has passed or a disease has disappeared.

One Sunday, when I was preparing this book, I asked our church members to write down a personal experience of healing and send it to me. A few of their letters suggested a lack of education or western 'sophistication' – or it may simply be that English is their second or third language. But regardless of education, language, age, sex or culture, they can surely be trusted when they say that a lump vanished after prayer, or that they can now see or hear more clearly, or that they can jump when before they could only totter, or that bleeding has stopped. Their analysis of the factors involved in the cure might be incomplete, their understanding of the healing process might be theologically simplistic, but their testimony to the basic fact of physical improvement is as reliable as that of a Harley Street surgeon.

The Gospels record Jesus healing quadriplegia, paraplegia, a severed ear, a withered hand, twelve blind eyes, eleven leprous bodies, two severe fevers, one gynaecological disorder, chronic curvature of the spine, dropsy, someone who was deaf and stuttered, someone who was paralysed and at the point of death, two people who had died, and a corpse which was fast decomposing.

The general statements add that he healed epileptics, set lame people walking, dumb people talking, and made cripples whole. Matthew 4:23–24 reports that Jesus '. . . went about all Galilee teaching in their synagogues, preaching the gospel of the kingdom, and healing all kinds of sickness and all kinds of disease among the people . . . and they brought to him all sick people who were afflicted with various diseases and torments, and those who were demon-possessed, epileptics, and paralytics; and he healed them.'

Jesus does not appear to have focused on healing ailments which were merely inconvenient, or could be healed by the primitive medicine of his day. Instead, he seems mainly to have cured acute suffering which caused isolation and loneliness; disorders which prevented social contact and employment; ailments which had persisted for long periods of time; and people near to either side of the point of death.

Cynics sometimes caricature the contemporary Pentecostal healing ministry as being concerned only with the bizarre and the trivial, with matters like leg-lengthenings and toothache. Even if this were true, the healings would be precious to the people who received them. However, in my experience, this caricature is wholly false.

I recognise that the experiences of healing which our church members submitted in response to my request are self-selecting and are therefore not necessarily a fully representative sample. But members testify that Christ has healed them, for example, from diseases of the spleen, liver, throat, stomach, bowels, brain, blood and heart; from high blood pressure, piles, lumbago, ovarian cysts, angina, pneumonia, malaria, asthma, infertility, cataracts, blindness, sickle-cell crisis, sinusitis, epilepsy, hernias, deafness, obsessive dieting and acute food allergies; from paralysis due to a stroke, the rejection of an artificial joint, electric shock, arthritis, a dislocated coccyx; from glands so swollen they were due to be surgically removed; from immobility and pain as the result of road accidents and industrial accidents; from growths, tumours and pain in every imaginable part of the body – and from many other very serious conditions.

The general statements in the Gospels which describe Jesus healing in front of large crowds of people are not first-century versions of contemporary, advertised healing services. Jesus did not seek the crowds. The crowds sought him. They came to inconvenient locations at unsociable times. They descended on a home where a miracle had occurred or gathered at a place where they knew Jesus to be. Although this is increasingly common in Africa, Asia and Latin America, we experience little like it in western Europe. Many of our modern meetings seem to be full of Christians seeking the latest in spiritual entertainment and bear little resemblance to those occasions in church history when the diseased and crippled have shuffled hopefully to a house where a believer was staying and pleaded for healing.

As well as healing at these sorts of informal gatherings, Jesus also went to people and healed them wherever they were. He delighted in healing beggars at the roadside, in healing ordinary working men and women in the course of their daily living, in healing outcasts and people with serious, socially disruptive, long-lasting conditions. Most of the reported miracles took place when Jesus was on a journey. Four people were healed in their homes, one in a garden, another at a dinner party, one at his funeral, another in his grave, one at a house meeting, another at a pool. Two of the people we are told about, however, were healed at organised religious meetings – in the local synagogue.

I suspect that one reason why some parts of the Church in Britain do not see the healings they hope for is because they are concentrating too much on ministry in meetings. Of course, God does care deeply about believers who are in some sort of pain but are still well enough to attend a celebration meeting, and, as we will see in Chapter 18, the Bible teaches the importance of pastoral healing. In our services almost every Sunday I see God easing pain and improving the ailments of believers, while some of our members rely as much on our weekly healing clinic as on their local GP.

Most of the testimonies submitted by our members, however, stated that they had been healed – or had been God's partner in healing – away from our meetings in each other's homes and in a multitude of different situations. Of course, the presence of Christ in our meetings means that many people are not disappointed when they come to a service expecting to experience some element of healing. But what happens at the meeting is often the last stage in a long process which involves many praying and caring people – as well as medication, doctors and nurses – most of whom are unaware of each other's contribution.

I believe that, somehow, we must seek to create many more evangelistic contexts for our ministries, that we must listen ever more intently for God's prompting to heal when we are away from meetings, and that we must intercede even more passionately for an outpouring of God's Spirit to help us reach ordinary working people and the social under-classes with God's love and healing power.

It is these people who often have least hope in this life and least access to medical resources. This means that God's healing power brings them a degree of hope which is hard for us to imagine – especially those of us who lead relatively comfortable lives and have little contact with our own society's poorer members.

The Gospels indicate that Jesus' healing miracles were, without exception, initiated in one of two different ways. He followed the pattern which had been established by the Old Testament prophets and set an example which we would do well to follow today.

In the New Testament, Jesus healed only in response to someone saying, 'Please heal me,' or 'Please heal my friend/servant/child'; or to God, by his Holy Spirit, ordering, 'Go heal that person.' In twelve of the twenty recorded healing encounters, the initiative was an unsolicited request – seven times by a friend or relative and five times by the individuals themselves. In the other encounters, it seems safe to conclude that the Father prompted Jesus to go to a particular individual and announce God's healing to that person.

The Gospels do not record Jesus healing all the sick people in Israel; but they do make it clear that he healed all those who came to him in faith asking for healing, and that he did heal particular individuals who were identified to him by the Father. If we believe that it really is God who is the divine healer, it surely makes sense for all our healing ministry to be initiated by him – either by God urging a person to request

God not a "principle"...

...ling from us, or by the Spirit instructing us to announce ...d's healing to a particular person. (I make several suggestions about how this works in practice in the last part of the book.)

Of course, there are so many healing promises in the Bible for believers that we can turn to the God who heals us any time we are unwell and be certain that he is willing to heal us. However, the scriptural healing promises do not mean that we should dash into the local hospital to pray for all the sick people in every ward! This was not Jesus' way.

I believe that operating outside God's way of initiating healing implies that we think we have some ability or power within us which enables us to heal whoever we like whenever we choose. I suspect that we would eliminate a great deal of unnecessary disappointment and false hope if we restricted our ministry activity to biblical principles. I know that it can rarely be wrong to offer to pray for somebody, but we need to remember that presumption is just as much a sin as disobedience.

**W**e have seen that the Old Testament prophets either interceded for healing or announced the imminent arrival of the healing. In the Gospels, Jesus, whose whole life was based in prayer, does not appear to have interceded publicly for the healing of any individual. John 5:19 shows he knew that he could do nothing by himself, but rather could do only what he saw the Father doing. Jesus restricted himself to doing whatever he understood the Father to be doing – and this seems to have been different with almost every healing encounter. Some leaders today seem to have predictable patterns of ministry, but this was not Jesus' way. When ministering healing, Jesus usually used a touch, or a spoken command, or an announcement – or a mixture of the three.

In the eleven of the twenty gospel encounters, Jesus touched the person to be healed. This was all he did in four cases, but at two of the resuscitations he added a word of command. On three occasions when he touched a person to be healed, Jesus also used saliva. In one example, he rebuked the illness before touching the person; and in another case, after casting out an evil spirit, he both announced the arrival of the healing and touched the person. Jesus healed two people who were several miles away from his physical presence and, in both cases, he gave a promise of healing. At five of the gospel encounters, Jesus spoke a command of healing without touching the person; and in three cases he instructed the people to do something which would help bring about their healing.

The story of the woman who touched the border of Jesus' garment stands out from the other healing stories. Rather than Jesus touching the woman, she touched him – and, instantly, he noticed power going out of him. It seems that the healing anointing was so strong upon Jesus that the woman's faith was enough to appropriate it. She reached out to Jesus, and God honoured her faith. That's exactly what happens today with us!

We would do well to learn from Jesus by saturating ourselves in preparatory prayer, discarding our techniques and traditions, and then ensuring that we do only what the Father says – for those to whom he sends us, and for those whom he sends to us.

*A*fter healing a person, Jesus often gave helpful personal advice and much-needed reassurance. We can see this, for example, in his instructions to Jairus to feed his daughter, and in his quick return to the John 9 beggar as soon as he heard about the man's excommunication.

All of the gospel stories are set against a backdrop of widespread wonder at Jesus' miracles and crowds flocking to hear him. In four of the stories, however, Jesus ordered the person who had been healed to tell nobody about the miracle: this 'secrecy' is a particular theme of Mark's Gospel. In doing this it seems that Jesus wanted to calm the excited Jewish crowds because they misunderstood the nature of his role as Messiah.

This misunderstanding was less likely among the Gentiles, hence Jesus' call for testimony in Mark 5:19. When the demon-possessed man in the country of the Gadarenes was free, 'Jesus said to him, "Go home to your friends, and tell them what great things the Lord has done for you, and how he has had compassion on you." And he departed and began to proclaim in Decapolis all that Jesus had done for him; and all marvelled.'

We will see in chapter twelve how healings are essentially signs which endorse God's word and point to his powerful and compassionate nature. Signs, however, can be ignored and a sensational healing does not necessarily convert anyone. Although the Gospels describe the crowds marvelling and wondering, they report spectators or relatives as being converted only in one of the healing encounters – John 4 reports that the nobleman and all his household believed when his son was restored to health. The Gospels make it clear that news of Jesus' miracles spread widely and quickly, and that the ordinary people admired Jesus and were awed by what they saw. In some cases, however, the Gospels show that the reaction was negative: twice there was persecution, once there was opposition and argument, and another time there were plots of destruction. The chief priests determined to kill Jesus after the raising of Lazarus, and in the Garden of Gethsemane their officials seized him as the high priest's servant grew a new ear. Most remarkably – yet the same thing still happens today – in five of the encounters, the Gospels report no reaction at all to Jesus' wonderful healings. It is as though some people are so busy – or so spiritually blind – that they do not see the sign.

Not even all the people who were healed in the Gospels began to follow and believe in Jesus. Peter's mother-in-law served Jesus; the John 9 beggar worshipped him; the nobleman's son believed in him; Bartimaeus was saved; but only one of the ten lepers returned to Christ. The other nine remained firmly unsaved.

Not everything was wonderful for all those who were healed. Some people were pestered with questions, the John 9 beggar was excommunicated, and Lazarus had a terrible time. From all over the area people rushed to gape at him, and the chief priests decided to assassinate him because of the numbers who were visiting him and wondering about Jesus!

We have seen that, throughout his earthly ministry, Jesus healed all the sick people whom his Father wanted to heal through him. But Jesus also made time to train his followers in his healing ministry. In the next chapter, we will look at the four Gospels and the book of Acts to see how well they learnt from their Lord – and to find out what we can learn from them.

# 7

# THE ANOINTED CHURCH

In the Old Testament, a staff was a symbol of prophetic authority. When Elisha sent his servant Gehazi to resuscitate a dead boy, he equipped him with his staff as the sign that Gehazi was acting in the name and authority of a true prophet. Gehazi had previously observed a healing miracle and had only to do exactly what his master had said. He did; yet nothing happened. Although he carried the symbol of Elisha's authority, Gehazi did not have Elisha's prophetic anointing and had not himself been anointed with the Spirit.

Jesus appears to have followed Elisha's pattern with his disciples. First, he ensured that they were with him when he healed the sick. Then – after they had spent many months watching him – Jesus invested them with his personal authority to cure the sick. This did not take the form of a wooden staff, instead they were given the right to speak in the power of Christ's own name. At this point, the disciples shared Jesus' personal authority, but they did not share his Holy Spirit anointing. Like Gehazi, they themselves had not been anointed with the Spirit.

Luke 8:22–9:6 shows how Jesus' twelve apostles were sent out on a healing mission after they had observed and experienced the calming of the storm, the deliverance of the Gerasene demoniac, the cure of the haemorrhaging woman, and the raising of Jairus' daughter. Matthew 10:1–16, Mark 3:13–19 and Luke 9:1–6 list Jesus' detailed instructions for their mission, with Matthew identifying the six pairs of apostles who worked together. They were told where to go, what to do, and how not to finance the trip. They went healing, casting

58

out demons and preaching the good news about the kingdom. At the end of their mission, they returned to Jesus to give him an account of all that had happened, and he withdrew with them to Bethsaida so that they could have time to themselves for prayer, rest and assessment.

Some time later, Christ expanded his healing ministry to include about another seventy disciples. Again they were sent out in pairs to definite locations with the instruction to heal and preach the good news. Doubtless they were much encouraged by Jesus' reassuring message that they would often feel as comfortable as sheep among wolves!

The Gospels do not record any specific details from these two trips, but Jesus' exasperated comment in Luke 9:40–41 comes just after the mission of the twelve apostles. 'How long shall I be with you and bear with you?' surely indicates that the apostles were not always completely successful in everything they attempted on Jesus' behalf!

We can say that, in his three years of earthly ministry, Jesus modelled and multiplied his healing ministry so that at least eighty people were involved. They healed in pairs, using the delegated authority of the name of Jesus. In Acts 1:4–5 and Luke 24:49 we read that, after his death and resurrection, Jesus urged them to stay in Jerusalem until they received the prophets' anointing with the Holy Spirit. Before Calvary, Jesus' disciples healed in the same way as Gehazi had tried to heal. After Pentecost, they healed in the same way as Elisha and Jesus – as full members of God's anointed, prophetic, interceding, healing community.

Before Pentecost, the anointing with the Holy Spirit was given to only a select few; since Pentecost, the Spirit's anointing has been freely available to all who are in Christ. The authority that the disciples had in Jesus' name was the same both before and after Pentecost. The dramatic change from their general ineffectiveness in the Gospels to their startling power in Acts can be put down to only two things: first, the difference made by their anointing with the Spirit at Pentecost; and, second, the spiritual consequences of the Son's death at Calvary.

The great test of any approach to the Christian healing ministry is how well it integrates the atonement and the anointing – Christ's great works at Calvary and Pentecost. Too many modern leaders stress one and ignore the other, whereas our understanding and practice of healing must surely be rooted in both together.

The great healing truth for believers today is that we can enjoy the victory over sickness which was won by Jesus on the cross, *and* that we have been given a share in the risen Christ's authority over all things, *and* that we can be anointed with the same Holy Spirit who directed and empowered the Son's earthly healing ministry. These are three threads of the one divine healing ministry – a ministry which is strongest when the threads are woven tightly together.

We live in and with the Holy Spirit only because of Christ's death, resurrection and ascension to heaven. We function as full members of God's anointed, prophetic, interceding, healing community, only because of what Jesus did at Calvary and at Pentecost. We experience forgiveness from sin and victory over sin because of the atoning cross, and we receive power to live and to witness through the pentecostal anointing.

These are not historical theories or pointless ideas, they are practical realities which can genuinely change our lives and the lives of hurting people around us. We all know people who ache for a healing touch from God. Please realise that he is willing to touch them, that he longs to touch them, but that he has chosen to touch them through a partner – through someone who has grasped the cross and is open to his Spirit; through someone who listens to God and is willing to face humiliation and rejection, as well as glory.

The stories we read in the Scriptures are not mere reminders of what God has done in the past, they are also signs which point to what he is doing today, and illustrations of what he longs to do through his Church – through you! The stories we are about to study in Acts could be your stories. The lame man at the temple gate could be the beggar you pass each day at the station. Peter's mother-in-law could be your difficult relative. Tabitha could be that elderly housebound saint in the next street. Saul could be that young man in the office who is always criticising the Church. Whenever we read a healing story in the Scriptures, we should remind ourselves that it typifies what God wants to do through us to some of the hurting people we meet.

The book of Acts records eight incidents of healing: (1) the lame man at the temple gate: 3:1–10; (2) blind Saul: 9:8–19; (3) paralysed Aeneas: 9:32–35; (4) dead Tabitha: 9:36–43; (5) the cripple at Lystra: 14:8–10; (6) stoned Paul: 14:19–20; (7) Eutychus: 20:7–12; (8) Publius' father: 28:7–8.

There are also seven general statements about healing in Acts: 2:43, 5:12–16, 6:8, 8:4–8, 14:3, 19:11–12, and 28:9. A careful reading of these passages shows how the early Church followed the general healing principles of the Old Testament prophets and Christ.

The people who were healed in Acts were a collection of beggars, social outcasts, opponents of the gospel, friends, and one elderly relative of the wealthy Prefect of Malta. Most of these people were healed of long-standing, serious, socially disruptive and economically disabling diseases – dysentery, death, paralysis, blindness and so on.

The healings took place in a wide variety of locations. One occurred on the way to a prayer meeting; three took place in a private house; one during an informal open-air meeting; and one in a field after violent persecution. The only healing to take place at a prearranged, regular meeting of the church was the recovery of Eutychus at the breaking of bread in Troas on the first day of the week.

The general statements about healing in Acts suggest that, like Jesus, the apostles ministered to all those who came to them requesting healing. Seven of the eight reported incidents demonstrate that the believers in the early Church were ready to minister when they recognised the Holy Spirit's prompting.

The middle-aged man of Acts 3, who had been lame since birth, always begged at the same temple gate. Peter and John must have passed him dozens of times, as must Jesus; yet the man was still paralysed. I am sure we can assume that he had never asked Jesus or any of his followers to heal him – all he wanted was money, he had no higher expectation.

We cannot know precisely how Peter was prompted to say what he said, but in some way the Holy Spirit informed him that the lame man was to be healed and that Peter was to speak the words. (We will look at learning to recognise God's voice and sensing the Spirit's prompting in Chapter 16.) I do not think that Peter and John had left home that morning intending to heal anybody, they were simply going to a prayer meeting. But when they walked past the sick man, they somehow sensed that they had to announce God's healing to him. They felt or heard the Spirit's prompting; they recognised that it was the Spirit and not their imagination or a demonic distraction; they obeyed God's voice – and God did the rest.

It is similar today. During meetings, I am always straining to pick up the quietest whispers of the Spirit about any people or ailments that the Father is wanting to heal. Sometimes I sense a word or name; at other times I feel a warmth or discomfort in a part of my body. I now understand that these feelings are God's way of showing me what he is wanting to do. One Wednesday evening last year, for example, I sensed during a midweek meeting that God was wanting to heal someone who had suffered an electric shock. I did not know the name, age, nationality, sex, or where or when the injury had occurred. God simply flashed the words 'electric shock' through my mind. So I announced that there was someone present at the meeting who had suffered an electric shock – either here or abroad – and that God was going to heal that person.

There were only about six hundred people present, but – unknown to me – a lady was there who had just returned from Ghana where she had suffered a shock in her right foot as a result of treading on the exposed wires of an iron. She still had a continuous burning sensation in her right leg and foot. That very afternoon a friend had insisted that she seek urgent medical help and she had promised to visit a doctor the following morning. Amazingly, that night, God chose to reveal her predicament to me and to heal her himself. Since that evening, she has had no more pain or discomfort in her leg.

Acts 9 shows us that God does not work in healing only through church leaders like Peter, but also through ordinary 'unknown' disciples like Ananias. He is an enigmatic figure, a local believer living in Damascus who was undoubtedly expecting to be arrested quite soon. We do not know if he had ever been God's partner in healing before meeting Saul, but it seems unlikely.

I think that the Holy Spirit has recorded Ananias' involvement to illustrate how God frequently uses even the most frightened and inexperienced disciples in wonderful healing. If, like God, we had known the possibilities of Saul's future and the extraordinary significance of this miracle, how many of us would have trusted such an inexperienced disciple? Most of us would have wanted to use Peter or one of the apostles. Instead, God chose an unknown novice as his partner – a pattern which he still commonly follows today.

I think that it is easy to understand why God uses men and women like Ananias. People have a tendency to want to follow and worship what they can see, and can focus too much on God's anointed healing partners and too little on the invisible, all-powerful God. When God works mainly through one or two gifted leaders, people tend – wrongly – to applaud and acclaim the man or woman of God. But when he works through a novice, it is obvious to everyone that it is God himself who is at work.

Ananias' vision was startling in its clarity and detail. He did not like what he thought he saw, and he told God so. In my experience, God rarely lets us know what will happen if we obey him. I have found that he normally expects us to obey him regardless of the consequences. Ananias, however, was a beginner, and God gave him an insight into what could happen through his unconditional obedience. What a struggle it must have been for Ananias to leave his home and walk to Straight Street to restore the sight of the man who held a warrant for his arrest!

Ananias was not a puppet, God did not make him visit Saul. Once Ananias recognised that the thoughts he sensed were God's voice, it was a straightforward matter of obedience. God would not work without his partner Ananias, and Ananias could not work independently of God. It is astonishing to contemplate the immense, eternal matters which hinged on whether or not Ananias would obey such a – to him – unprecedented order.

Most of us rarely grasp the extent to which God relies on our partnership, and we seldom so much as glimpse the considerable consequences of our obedience.

Aeneas had been bedridden with paralysis for eight years when he was visited by Peter. Their encounter does not appear to be anything other than part of Peter's regular pastoral visitation of the disciples, and it is impossible to tell from the Scriptures whether there had been any previous healings in Lydda – though I doubt it. Peter stood over Aeneas and sensed that God was about to cure this particular paralytic. Peter had been anointed with the Holy Spirit at Pentecost, and this 'sensing' or prompting was merely God keeping his Amos 3:7–8 promise. So Peter prophetically announced what he had just sensed from the Spirit. Peter did not heal Aeneas, or even hint that he had healed him. Peter's part in the healing process was simply to announce the wonderful news to Aeneas: 'Jesus Christ heals you. Arise and make your bed.'

Within a few days, two visitors arrived from Joppa, some twelve miles away on the coast. They brought news that a beloved saint had died and many were greatly distressed. And they begged for a pastoral visit as quickly as possible. Returning immediately with them, Peter was taken straight to Tabitha's body. Coming as it did, so soon after the miracle at Lydda, it is surely likely that Tabitha's death would have caused Peter to turn over in his mind the possibility of Tabitha being raised from the dead. The first thing that Peter did was to kneel and pray in privacy. The Scriptures do not record whether his prayer was a petition for guidance, boldness or a miracle. But whatever he prayed, when Peter rose from his knees he knew what he had to do.

A long-life cripple sat in a crowd listening to Paul preach the good news. Somehow the Holy Spirit so worked in the man during Paul's sermon that he had the faith to be healed. We do not know quite what happened – perhaps Paul was preaching about Jesus the healer – but somehow Paul's attention was drawn to the cripple. He watched him closely, could see 'faith' written all over the man's face, and broke off in mid-sermon to call out a healing command.

As a result of the miracle, Paul first received acclamation

and then persecution. The crowd hurled boulders at him and dragged his unconscious body out of Lystra towards the town cemetery. Yet within a short while Paul was striding back to town, and the next day he was well enough to walk thirty miles to Derbe.

The book of Acts glosses over what happened. It mentions that disciples gathered round the body, but does not say whether they prayed, announced healing, touched the body, or whether God worked sovereignly without any human partners. We miss the point if we are concerned to establish a technique which we then hope to copy. Doubtless the disciples' faith would have been high because of the earlier miracle, and many would have prayed enthusiastically. But the miracle occurred because of God's power and compassion – not because the disciples passed some sort of healing examination.

The weekly meeting at Troas was a long one – longer even than most of ours at Kensington Temple! The local disciples met to break bread and then Paul preached a lengthy farewell sermon. Eutychus (remarkably, his name means lucky!) was seated on the window sill; he grew drowsy, fell asleep, and toppled out of the window to fall three floors to the ground. Most people thought that Eutychus was dead, including – apparently – Doctor Luke. But Paul had other information. He was prompted by the Spirit to take action and announce life.

The final healing incident reported in Acts took place on Malta. Paul visited the Prefect's father, who was ill with dysentery. We do not know what Paul prayed – whether it was for guidance or a miracle – but after praying Paul knew what God was going to do and what he had to do. He obeyed the Spirit's prompting, placed his hands on the sick man, and the man was healed. The news spread, and Paul was soon faced with a large number of sick islanders asking to be healed. God continued to work through Paul, and they were all healed too.

The stories in Acts suggest that Christians in the early Church often spoke words of command when they were partnering God in his healing work. In Acts 3, Peter commanded, 'In the name of Jesus Christ of Nazareth, rise up and walk.' He then lifted the man to his feet and let go! Ananias announced, 'The Lord Jesus has sent me that you may receive your sight,' and immediately Paul could see. Peter declared, 'Aeneas, Jesus Christ heals you; arise and make your bed.' And he commanded the body of Tabitha, 'Arise.' Paul yelled at the cripple, 'Stand up straight on your feet.' He clasped Eutychus to himself and prophetically announced, 'Do not trouble yourself, for his life is in him.' Only with Publius' father does touch seem to have been used without a command or announcement of healing.

The general statements in Acts 5:12 and 19:11 are not unlike the story of the woman who touched the border of Jesus' garment. Aprons and handkerchiefs which had touched Paul were taken to the sick, and the Jerusalem and district incurables tried to position themselves so that some portion of Peter's shadow passed over them as he walked by. Luke, the author of Acts, suggests that the faith which is implicit in this behaviour was honoured by God. Perhaps, also, the healing anointing was so strong upon Peter and Paul at these times that – as with Elisha's bones – it was almost something tangible which was capable of being passed on. It does appear that, sometimes, there is a residual or lingering effect when God works in unusual power. When I returned to Nyota Farm, three years after tasting revival there, I learnt that handkerchiefs and clothing brought to the meetings were taken to sick people in the area with phenomenal results.

*A*cts reports that the healing miracles we have considered played a significant role in evangelism and early church growth, even though many of them occurred in a pastoral context. After healing the lame man, Peter and John were arrested, imprisoned and reprimanded by the rulers; but many of those who heard Peter's explanation of the miracle became believers. Saul's healing led on to his extremely fruitful future. When Aeneas was healed, 'all who dwelt at Lydda and Sharon saw him and turned to the Lord'; and the whole of Joppa heard about Tabitha's resuscitation, 'and many believed on the Lord'.

However, not all the incidents had a great evangelistic impact. The healing of the cripple in Lystra led to misunderstanding and persecution. The people were 'greatly encouraged' by Eutychus' recovery, but nobody is reported as being saved. And though many requested healing after the healing of Publius' father, Acts does not mention any conversions.

I am sure that we all have very much to learn from the healing early Church, but attempts just to implement the pattern and technique of the first Christians are surely inadequate. It is vital that we receive, as they received, the prophets' anointing with the Spirit, without which we are as impotent as Gehazi.

Yet there are many modern believers – leaders even – who have received that anointing but who do not see God endorse their words with healing miracles. Perhaps we also need to examine the two main contexts within which Jesus and the early Church functioned as God's healing partners, and ask ourselves whether our healing ministry would benefit from being set against a similar background.

# 8

# HOPE FOR THE POOR

When Jesus introduced himself in the Nazareth synagogue as the fulfilment of Isaiah 61:1–2, he made it clear that he had a special concern to reach out to the poor. Luke 4:18–19 reports that Jesus introduced his ministry with these words, 'The Spirit of the Lord is upon me, because he has anointed me to preach the gospel to the poor. He has sent me to heal the broken-hearted, to preach deliverance to the captives and recovery of sight to the blind, to set at liberty those who are oppressed, to preach the acceptable year of the Lord.'

Clearly this is an important statement by Jesus, and we can think of it as his 'manifesto' or 'mission statement'. In this passage he summarises the purpose of his anointing as 'preaching the gospel *to the poor*', and then provides five examples of what this means in practice. This shows us that 'healing the broken-hearted' and 'releasing the oppressed' are not different – or even complementary – activities to 'preaching the gospel to the poor'; instead, they are that preaching in action. It also shows us that 'the captives' (the Greek word implies prisoners-of-war) and 'the blind' are not distinct groups from 'the poor'; rather, they are aspects of being poor.

Many Christian leaders disagree about the identity of 'the poor' whom Jesus was anointed to reach. Most evangelicals argue that he meant the spiritually poor, while other leaders insist that Jesus was referring to the politically or financially poor. I think, however, that their understandings miss the point of Jesus' manifesto. The Greek word *ptochos*, which most versions of the Bible translate as *poor*, literally means 'someone who is cowering down or hiding for fear'. A few modern Bibles

68

helpfully reflect this by referring to 'the afflicted' instead of 'the poor', and I believe that we can best appreciate this today by thinking in terms of 'the hurting' rather than 'the poor'. This means that Jesus was not anointed to preach the gospel mainly to those who have few material or financial resources. Instead, he was anointed to preach the good news to those who are afflicted and hurting; to those who are broken-hearted, blind, imprisoned and oppressed. His healing anointing really does mean hope for a hurting world.

We should think about this 'gospel hope for the hurting' in three overlapping ways, for Jesus was anointed to preach the gospel to those who are afflicted by sin, by Satan and by society. Sin hurts people, and the consequences of sin include emotional pain, broken relationships and wounded lives. Men and women are afflicted by sin; they are blinded, oppressed and held captive by sin. And Jesus was anointed to preach the gospel of hope to all who are being hurt by sin.

It is the same with Satan. He is the deceiver and destroyer of humanity. He is an evil defamer and a despotic ruler. People are held captive by him as 'prisoners-of-war' and he feeds on their fear and distress. Jesus was anointed to announce the good news of freedom to all who are afflicted by Satan, and Acts 10:38 reports how Jesus' anointing meant that he healed all who were oppressed by the devil.

But our concern must not stop at sin and Satan. We must go on to see that society also deeply afflicts and hurts people. Large numbers of men and women are financially, politically and emotionally destitute because of the way that society works. It oppresses and isolates people. It blinds them to justice and truth. It devalues and depersonalises them. It breaks their hearts, steals their hope, strips them of their humanity and holds them captive to its false values. And Jesus was anointed to preach the gospel of acceptance to those who are hurting because of society's actions and attitudes, as well as to those who are in the grip of sin.

Jesus made this 'society' element clear in the last part of his manifesto by stating that he had been anointed 'to preach the acceptable year of the Lord'. This was a direct reference to the 'year of jubilee', the year of liberation among men and women appointed by God and described in Leviticus 25. This prescribed a social revolution which was supposed to be held every fifty years. During every jubilee year, fields lay fallow, people returned to their own homes, land was restored to its original owner, debts were cancelled and slaves set free. For people who were afflicted by society, especially for those who were homeless and in debt, Jesus' announcement of 'the acceptable year of the Lord' would have been the best possible news they could hear.

All this should help us to appreciate that 'preaching the gospel to the poor' does not essentially mean preaching to the naked and starving overseas, or even to the growing numbers of destitute people in western Europe. Instead, it primarily means reaching out to the great mass of ordinary people who are afflicted by sin, by Satan and by society.

We can understand this by looking at Jewish society in Jesus' day and by seeing whom the Gospels describe Jesus as reaching. There were three primary social groups in first-century Israel. First, there was a small group of educated and powerful people, the political and religious leaders, who had tremendous influence over the rest of the population. Second, there was the vast bulk of ordinary people who had hardly any education, were almost completely powerless and had little control over their own lives. And, third, there was a small group of beggars and social outcasts who were rejected by everyone else.

Our modern financial understanding of 'poverty' has led many to assume that Jesus had the third group in mind when he referred to 'the poor'. But the Gospels show that it was the second group, 'the common people', who heard him gladly, that it was the vast bulk of ordinary, seemingly unimportant, working people whom he focused on reaching.

The ordinary people of Jesus' day were afflicted by their Roman conquerors, by the Jewish religious authorities, by double and corrupt taxation, by their sense of powerlessness and insignificance, and by all the ordinary pressures of their short lives. And Jesus came among them with the revolutionary messages that, 'you matter', 'you're valuable', 'you're import-ant', 'you're significant', 'you're accepted', 'you're forgiven', 'your freedom is coming, for this is God's jubilee year'. Jesus overlooked their lack of status and education, appreciated their true eternal worth, and upset the social conventions of this day by treating them as the equals of the educated, powerful elite.

Of course, Jesus was not anointed to preach only to 'the common people', as the Gospels also describe him reaching out to affluent and influential people who were hurting in some way, like Nicodemus, Joseph of Arimathea, Levi, Joanna, Susanna, Zacchaeus and the rich young ruler. We have already seen, as well, that over 60 per cent of Jesus' healing miracles involved the afflicted people who were right at the edge of Jewish society.

Personally, I am sure that we share Jesus' calling if we have received his anointing. He came to find the lost, to heal the broken-hearted, to give sight to the blind, to preach the gospel to the poor. His ministry reached out to the most obviously hurting people in his society, and so – I suggest – should ours. Obviously, the phrases of Luke 4:18 do have a spiritual application – Jesus did come for the spiritually lost, the spiritually imprisoned, the spiritually blind, the spiritually poor, and so on. However, the scriptural accounts of Jesus' ministry show that he also meant these phrases literally, for the religious leaders of his day were continually affronted by the way that he welcomed, ate with and ministered to beggars, lepers, tax-collectors, women with 'certain reputations' and unclean sinners.

I believe this means that we should be as focused as Jesus on ministering God's forgiveness, acceptance and healing to the people who live at the fringes of modern life – as well as to more prosperous people and ordinary men and women who are outside the Church. I know that God loves affluent and educated believers, and is very willing to heal them, but I think we must ensure that his healing compassion is felt today as widely as it was in first-century Israel. As we have seen, this means that we must reach out with our healing anointing to all who are afflicted and hurting, to the alienated young, to the isolated elderly, to the homeless, to the unemployed, to immigrant groups, to ethnic minorities and, especially, to the humble poor.

This has huge implications for church life and mission. The majority of modern church leaders are graduates who find it easiest to reach out to people like them. Most of our church services and evangelistic methods are geared to reaching and discipling the educated, those who are at home in the world of ideas and words. In western Europe today, most churches are elitist groups whose members are educated, affluent and professional. Somehow, we have to recognise that we have been anointed to preach the gospel to the afflicted, to the bulk of the population who live on housing estates, read tabloid newspapers, enjoy watching TV soaps and game shows, drink beer, smoke cigarettes, play the lottery and take package holidays.

The Christian books and magazines we currently produce do not reach them. Most of our sermons are not comprehensible to them. Our services are not relevant to their culture. Too many of us do not easily relate to ordinary people: we look down on them, we are amused by their values, we are disparaging towards their culture. If we are to preach the gospel effectively to 'the poor', we will need to repent about many of our attitudes, allow God's unpatronising compassion to overwhelm us, and learn how we can reach the afflicted and hurting people of our day with the good news of the acceptable year of the Lord.

Luke 4:18 shows us that Jesus was anointed with the Holy Spirit to reach the poor essentially by preaching the gospel. Although healing miracles do provide genuine lasting hope, they are only signs which point people to God and his gospel. We must not forget that the healing God himself, not healing miracles, is the great hope for all humanity. The ministry of healing, therefore, needs to be set in contexts which enable ordinary people to grasp the reality towards which the sign points.

There are two main New Testament contexts for the healing ministry. First, the proclamation of the gospel to people who are poor, to men and women who are afflicted and hurting. And, second, a lifestyle which facilitates this proclamation by ensuring that we are focused on the afflicted, are relevant

72

to their needs, and are personally accessible to them.

Jesus was anointed by the Spirit to preach the gospel to the poor, and he lived among them in a way which showed that God accepted and loved them. His healing miracles confirmed the good news that he taught about forgiveness, and demonstrated the divine love that his living among them suggested. Clearly, these are not the only scriptural contexts for healing, but they have such a high New Testament profile that we must consider their implications for the contemporary healing ministry.

We have seen that the prophets' anointing with the Spirit in the Old Testament equipped them for the ministries of intercession and healing. We must recognise, however, that their anointing was given principally to inspire and empower them to pass on the word of the Lord and to call people back to the true God. In the same way, Jesus' anointing was given for the main purpose of speaking God's words, but it also involved healing, deliverance and intercession. Equally, our anointing with the Holy Spirit, which since Pentecost has been freely available to all believers, is also given so that we may make Jesus better known – it provides power for witnessing accurately and effectively to Jesus.

When Jesus began to speak in the Nazareth synagogue, he won the initial approval of all his listeners, for they were astonished by his gracious words. 'Is this not Joseph's son?' was their question: they were puzzled by the change in Jesus' speaking. Throughout his ministry, it was always Jesus' words which made the greatest impression – because of the authority and power with which he spoke. The healing miracles were signs pointing to God's compassion and power, but they also confirmed what Jesus said. They illustrated what he announced – that the kingdom of God had come among them in power and that it was wide open to everyone, even to despised sinners. I do not believe that the anointed ministry of divine healing can be entirely removed from this context of 'preaching the gospel to the poor' without some distortion of both the message and the miracle.

The twelve apostles were sent out by Jesus to proclaim the

kingdom of God, to heal the sick and to cast out demons. The charges were parallel and inseparable. They went from village to village announcing the good news and healing. Then Jesus sent out another seventy or so disciples with the same mission: they were to cure the sick and announce that the kingdom of God had come. When they returned with joy, they reported that even demons had submitted when they used Jesus' name.

The early Christians kept these callings together. They preached and they healed. Whenever someone was healed, a spoken explanation was offered which pointed to Jesus. This was one of the central secrets of the Church's phenomenal growth. In Acts, church growth is attributed fourteen times to the association between signs, wonders and the preaching of the gospel. In six places, the growth of the Church is precipitated by signs and wonders alone. Only once, at Corinth, is church growth possibly related to preaching alone, but Paul's reference to 'demonstrations of power' in 1 Corinthians 2:4 could easily include miracles. This should be enough to convince us that the proclamation of the good news is a critical biblical context for healing.

Very few of the people offered as examples of healing in the New Testament were followers of Jesus. Paul, Lazarus and Tabitha were disciples – and, perhaps, so too were Aeneas, Eutychus and Peter's wife's mother – but the other thirty-two people do not appear to have been Jesus' followers at the time of their healing. Some of them may have been interested or curious, many of them certainly believed that Jesus could cure them, but they were not committed disciples: they had not forsaken all to follow him.

If we sincerely long to partner God in his healing ministry, we will do well not to overlook this principle. When we look back on the previous twelve months of our ministry, we need to ask ourselves several questions. Have most of the people we have ministered healing to been believers or the unsaved? What percentage were from the poorer groups of society? Have most of the settings for our healing ministry been evangelistic, worship or pastoral? Has most of our ministry been in or outside meetings?

74

As we have seen, this emphasis on an evangelistic context for healing does not mean that there is no place either for pastoral healing or for healing in regular worship services. These are important elements of the Church's ministry of healing, and we will focus on them in later chapters. However, it does mean that our healing ministry should reflect the scriptural focus on the unsaved, especially on reaching the unbelieving poor with the gospel, and going out to heal them wherever they are.

I am certain that one of the main reasons why there are not many more clear examples of healing in churches today is that it has often been separated from evangelism, isolated from ordinary people, and imprisoned in church meetings. If Jesus commissioned us go out preaching and healing, how dare we not heal – or not go out! Can we really expect God to bless us when we fail to obey his most simple directions?

We also need to recognise the second main context – that Jesus had to move among the afflicted in order to be able to preach the gospel and announce God's healing to them. He did not come from heaven with all the obvious splendour and public acclaim to which, as God, he was entitled. He did not live in an emperor's palace and issue anointed instructions from a distance. Instead, he demonstrated his identification with humanity by living as an ordinary man and by being subject to exactly the same pressures as everyone else.

Jesus lived in a way to which the hurting people of his day could relate. He ate their food, stayed in their homes, listened to their concerns, and was available to them. He befriended prostitutes, alcoholics, terrorists, the terminally ill and those who were financially corrupt. He embraced lepers, washed dirty feet, went without sleep, was often misunderstood – and he preached and he healed and he cast out demons. Again, I do not believe that the anointed ministry of divine healing can be entirely removed from this context of 'living the gospel among the poor' without some distortion of both the message and the miracle.

Jesus did not commission the twelve apostles only to preach

the gospel, to heal the sick and to cast out demons. He also instructed them to do these things from within a distinctive lifestyle of relative simplicity. They were to take nothing for the journey, no staff or bag, no bread or money, not even a change of clothes. This meant that they had to depend on God to provide them with healing power *and* material provision, that they had to free themselves from unnecessary distractions and focus entirely on their calling, and that they could not isolate themselves from the people they were trying to reach.

We know that Jesus exchanged the glory of heaven for the hardships of earth, and that – when he started to preach and to heal – he turned away from the relative security of his family home. He preached and healed with no hope of any earthly reward. He called people to turn away from mammon, so he did not demand a fee or insist on a love-offering – though he willingly accepted the generous support and hospitality of many wealthy people. He taught his followers not to worry about material provision and to rely completely on the Father to define and to meet all their material needs. He lived in a way which was relevant to the ordinary people he was trying to reach, a way which ensured that he was available to them and which enabled them to identify easily with him. Jesus perfectly demonstrated a life lived in dependence upon God for everything. He trusted his Father for food, clothes, direction, words *and* healing power; and he called his disciples to follow in his footsteps.

When Jesus sent out the seventy disciples, he selected them from among those who had followed him on the understanding that a fox appeared to have greater financial security than his disciples. Like the twelve apostles, the seventy were also instructed to 'carry neither purse, sack, nor sandals' and to consume what they were given on their mission. These orders meant that they were totally focused on their mission, fully involved with the people they were trying to reach, and not distracted by material worries or personal special interests.

Luke 22:35–38 makes it clear that Jesus' followers never lacked anything on their evangelistic healing tours, but it also shows that their instructions were varied to reflect a change in circumstances. Here Jesus prepared his followers for a hostile future and more extended times of ministry. They might not be offered hospitality any more so now they would need to take a purse with them to pay for their food. This reminds us that we should not attempt simplistically to apply an isolated verse, but rather that we should study the whole Scriptures and live by the principles they teach.

The testimony of Acts makes it clear that Christians in the early Church continued to preach and to heal in the context of lives which were radical, relevant and attractive to the people they were trying to reach. There were no legalistic demands; instead, the Jerusalem converts willingly owned everything in common, sold their goods and possessions, and shared out the proceeds among themselves according to what each one needed. Peter and John must have set a shining example as, in Acts 3:6, they had no money to give to the lame man – so they healed him instead!

M any Christian leaders in western Europe wonder why there are, at present, so many more healing miracles in Africa, Asia and Latin America. It is true that there is much more faith and far less cynicism in the Church on those continents, but it is not clear whether the miracles the Christians are experiencing are responsible for their greater faith or whether their faith has contributed to the miracles. We all know how hard it is for us to respond when preachers exhort us to have more faith – and how quickly our faith rises without any effort when miracles are happening around us!

What is also true, however, is that in many sections of the Church on these continents we can see the features we have been considering. They are experiencing healing miracles; they do have a great passion for evangelistic mission; they are reaching out to ordinary, less-educated, powerless groups; and – in the main – they are living among the people they are trying to reach in a way which is relevant to their lives. They may not always consciously be seeking to apply the principles behind Jesus' instructions to the twelve and the seventy, but they are usually ministering healing to those who know that they are afflicted within the contexts of mission and dependence on God to provide their needs.

Those of us who have been placed by God in developed, more affluent nations, have to live in the tension of knowing the gulf between our position and the plight of so many poor and hurting people overseas. The simple fact that we have flush toilets, hot water on tap, a choice of food and clothing, even that we have access to so many affordable books and can actually read them, means that most of us are 'millionaires' in global terms. We might not be able to do very much about the appalling inequalities of our world, but we should never become complacent or accepting about them. Instead, I believe that we can ask the Spirit to help us discover our own creative way of living in some sort of meaningful identification with our brothers and sisters overseas – and with the increasing numbers of people in our own land who are desperately poor and socially isolated.

The example of the incarnation is always before us. The Word became flesh – Jesus sacrificed the glory of heaven to live among us and experience our struggles and disappointments. But his living among us was never patronising, rather it was immensely practical as he sought to reveal God's nature and to reconcile us to God. Jesus did this by the way that he lived, *and* by preaching and healing.

Somehow, like Jesus, we have to be deeply involved with our own generation and yet remain tightly focused on our particular spiritual calling. We need to live in a way which is culturally relevant and highly accessible to the people we have been called to reach – while resisting the pressures of materialism and consumerism and rejecting the advances of so many worthy but less-than-the-best activities. It is too easy for us to slip into lifestyles which are either indistinguishable from the unbelievers around us or so different from them that we cease to be relevant and accessible. We will never be effective in reaching the great mass of ordinary people if we live in a way which isolates us from them.

I do not believe that our anointing to preach the gospel to 'the poor' means that we must live in a way which celebrates poverty. Jesus might call a few of his disciples to sell all their possessions and give the proceeds away, but he has anointed us to reach the poor, not to be poor. Instead, I believe that living to facilitate the preaching of the gospel to ordinary people means developing contentment, eliminating clutter, giving sacrificially, repudiating materialism, and ensuring we are free from distractions so that we can focus on God's work. It means putting people first and ensuring that hurting men and women and children of every background are comfortable with us – whether they are hungry and homeless, wealthy and complacent, educated and articulate, or ordinary working people who may find it difficult to express themselves clearly. Our reason for living among people in this straightforward way should be to show them what God is like and to encourage them to be reconciled to God. We do this by the way we live *and* by preaching, healing and casting out demons.

At Kensington Temple we are deeply committed to church planting and are eager to learn from others involved in this work around the world. One of my friends has closely studied the first waves of church planting in western Europe, and he often encourages me to learn from the early preaching monks who first reached Europe with the message of Christ and planted churches in almost every village across the continent.

Many monastic orders began as movements of God's Spirit. The monks committed themselves to prayer, simple preaching and a life stripped of distractions so that they could focus completely on their mission. Most modern evangelicals and Pentecostals imagine that the early monks isolated themselves socially and had no passion for evangelism. Yet if that were true, they would not have brought Christianity to village after village across Europe. Records claim that, at first, God confirmed their words with many miraculous healings and that these were one of the key reasons for their church-planting effectiveness. They were also deeply committed to caring for the sick and dying, and to developing the primitive medicine of their day.

As the years went by, these movements were distracted by

mammon, ruined by legalism, and destroyed by false doctrine. Members of monastic communities stopped preaching the true gospel and started living in a comfortable way which isolated them from the ordinary people around them – and all credible reports of miracles ceased.

In a similar way, the great evangelical missionary movements of the last two centuries linked living among needy people with preaching and healing. Although most non-pentecostal missionaries did not seek healing miracles, their commitment to medical healing and evangelistic preaching was a key reason for their extraordinary effectiveness. They preached, they healed, they tried to live in a way which was relevant to the people around them, and they tried to reach out to the poorest groups in the community. As the present-day churches in Africa, Asia and Latin America are – to a considerable extent – the fruit of these pioneering medical gospel missions to the poor, it should not surprise us that these churches are vibrant healing, preaching communities which put the British Church to shame.

In the second half of the twentieth century, it was the radical Pentecostals around the world who were in the forefront of preaching and healing. It is now widely accepted that the fastest growth in the world-wide Church is among Pentecostal-based churches in Africa, Asia and Latin America – and these are those who generally emphasise the biblical principles and contexts we have considered.

Most believers in the less developed nations do have a view of the world which is wide open to supernatural signs and wonders. This is clearly a factor in their rich experience of healing, but not, perhaps, the only one. I suspect other important factors are the way that they focus the healing ministry on reaching ordinary working people, set it in the context of evangelism, stress the need for the anointing of the Spirit, and lead uncluttered lives which are accessible and relevant to the poor of their lands.

Some leaders suggest that we will enter into the African and Latin American blessing as soon as we adopt their world view. I wonder whether this is naively optimistic and the truth more complex. It would be equally valid to suggest that British churches will move from praying for the sick to seeing God heal the sick when we ensure that we focus more on reaching ordinary hurting people, when Pentecostal evangelism is central to all our activities, and when we develop people-centred, non-materialistic lives which do not distract us from the work of God's kingdom.

# 9

# HEALING EMPHASES

In a church like Kensington Temple, there are often visitors who come hoping to see the sick being supernaturally healed by God. If they attend one or two services, they are usually encouraged by what they see, but they are not really with us long enough to grasp *why* people are being healed.

In earlier chapters, we looked at the Scriptures to see *how* God heals and to understand the contexts of healing that he favours; we also, however, need to develop a mature grasp of the theory behind biblical healing. Some readers may find the next few chapters slightly harder work, but please resist the temptation to leap over the teaching. Believers who are only concerned with pragmatic questions about the practical reality of miracles can be misled by unbalanced emphases on particular aspects of healing.

I have observed that healing seems to become an end in itself for some believers, and that they can be devastated when there is a lack of healing. But God himself should be the great pursuit of our lives, not any of his gifts. We read in Luke 10:17–20 that Jesus rebuked the disciples for celebrating the miracles that they had seen, and told them that they should be rejoicing because their names were written in heaven – their relationship with God was more important than any miracle they had seen. We can handle the temporary disappointments and difficult circumstances of this life far better when we are genuinely seeking the living God with every fibre of our being. Nevertheless, we should be eager to move into and in his healing because it really is available to us. We are not justified in ignoring healing just because other things are more important.

I believe that our understanding of healing should be firmly rooted in the full biblical picture of God's redemptive work. People are less likely to become unbalanced about healing when they realise that it is only one part of the total process of God working out his salvation in his groaning creation. Divine healing is available, and it is available not only because God is the creator but also because healing is a distinctive part of his full redemptive process which runs backwards into our past and forwards to the great and final day before us.

Many believers' mental struggles with healing ease when they grasp that it is a sub-section of salvation. All evangelical and Pentecostal believers are taught that they have been saved, that they are being saved, and that they will be saved. It is the same with healing. There is much that we have experienced and there is so much more that we can experience, but we will be frustrated and puzzled if we fail to recognise, and to emphasise, the important fulfilment of earthly divine healing which will occur when we are transformed at the day of resurrection.

Since the beginning of time, all the people who have experienced a greater or lesser degree of divine healing have gone on to die. Even the people whom Jesus resuscitated only survived for the rest of their 'natural' life spans. Sadly, some of the Kenyans miraculously healed at Nyota Farm were maimed and killed in civil unrest just a few years later. On earth, the fact of death means that no healing can ever be permanent and absolute. No matter how wonderful, every healing only delays the process of ageing and dying. However, every healing, every victory over sickness, is also a foretaste of the final destruction of sickness and of our total transformation on the last day.

In Christ, through the cross, we know that death has been defeated and we will be healed – really healed, eternally and perfectly healed – at the day of resurrection. It is not wrong to promise this resurrection transformation as the fulfilment of healing, for this is the great hope without which there must ultimately be earthly despair. It is wrong to suggest, however, that we cannot experience divine healing 'here and now', and it is also wrong to suggest that divine healing is either 'now or then'. It is 'here and now *and* then'!

We know that God does not forgive us either now or then. He forgives us now, and this is a foretaste, and a guarantee, of the forgiveness we will experience at the last day. By grace, through faith, we have received a genuine and tangible experience of divine forgiveness which has dramatically changed our lives. But we recognise that we are still troubled by sin and look to the final day for the fulfilment of God's redemptive work. We do not tie ourselves in theological knots worrying about the now and then aspects of forgiveness: instead, we rejoice in them; we recognise that they are part and parcel of his great work of salvation; and our present experience enables us to look forward with enormous hope. It is the same with healing.

The Bible is packed with promises of healing, and we need to grasp that these are for fulfilment in this life – for we will not need healing in the life to come. The startling truth is that there will not be any healing in heaven, because there will be no need for healing then. So it is ridiculous for people to suggest that the biblical promises of healing are all for the future. There is no evidence that Jesus ever told anyone to wait for the resurrection for their healing – he healed people then and there, while they were alive on earth. In the same way, in Romans 8:10–11 Paul promises life for our 'mortal' bodies not for our 'resurrected' bodies.

It is wonderful, God really does want us to experience his healing today. In this life, however, there will always be areas of his redemptive work where our knowledge and experience are imperfect and we must patiently await completion or fulfilment at the final day. Rather than plunging into despair at the thought of waiting for fulfilment, we should thank God for the foretaste – and plead with the Spirit for an intensification of our experience of the foretaste.

It seems to me that, although there are many subtly different approaches within the Church to the *how* of divine healing, there are three distinctive ideas about the *why* of healing. These can be roughly categorised according to the emphasis they give to the different members of the Trinity. Of course I recognise that few believers subscribe entirely to any one of the approaches I describe. In reality, most of us are loosely based in one but we also embrace various aspects from the other two. I think it is helpful, however, to analyse the distinctive approaches to divine healing so that we can see their particular strengths and weaknesses, and can begin to draw the best of them together.

One approach focuses on the Father and stresses the full and overriding sovereignty of God. Believers from this tradition can usually be identified by their use of the expression, 'If it be your will' – which they seem to use almost every time they pray about the healing of the sick. They look to a verse like Ephesians 1:11 and believe that God only heals today when he chooses – if he chooses. They do not really believe God will choose to heal very often in the present, and they confuse God's will to heal and God's willingness to heal.

This approach stresses that almighty God is in complete control, and that – as in the story of Job – any sickness or injury is part of God's permissive will. Leaders in this tradition question the idea of a contemporary healing ministry which embraces the idea of God's power dynamically breaking through to touch people physically and emotionally. Instead, they focus on God's full future healing for believers at the final day. There is virtually no concept of divine healing as part of the Church's evangelistic mission, and little practical expectation of healing for anyone in the here and now.

We dare not dismiss the sovereignty of God, for there clearly are times of blessing and seasons of barrenness. God does heal one and not another, here and not there, and he does not need to explain his actions to us. Equally, any stress on God himself being the healer is always a helpful corrective to the foolish excess of attention which is often lavished upon human ministers of healing. This emphasis on the Father's sovereignty, however, is not the full picture. It says nothing about the place of healing in evangelism, nothing about our partnership with God, and nothing about God's willingness to heal – which means that it misrepresents God's character. It ignores the critical biblical fact that only those who have been anointed with the Spirit are involved in healing. It unhelpfully glamorises sickness, often wrongly associating it with suffering due to opposition and persecution, and it overlooks the central point that sickness was dealt with by Christ on the cross. This healing emphasis does not adequately explain why everyone who came to Jesus was healed, or why so many people are healed today, or why the Bible links healing with preaching, the Spirit's anointing and salvation.

The great weakness of the sovereignty approach is that it lacks faith. Jesus' approving comments about the faith of the centurion and the woman who touched him are ignored. His response to the disciples – that unbelief was the reason for their lack of healing – is forgotten. The statement in Mark 6:5–6 is overlooked. According to this approach, it is God or nothing. We have no part. Faith is not looked for either in those healed or in those ministering. And, because it is faith which feeds hope, this leads to a depressing lack of hope for those believers who are nurtured in this emphasis.

*A* second approach to healing focuses on the Son. It thinks about the *why* of healing, and stresses the complete atonement of the cross. The word 'atonement' comes from the Hebrew word for 'cover' and refers to everything Jesus achieved at the cross. As Jesus not only covered our sins but also completely removed them, 'atonement' is not always an accurate word to describe Christ's full saving work. However, I use it here because it has become established as the word for this healing approach.

Believers in the atonement healing tradition can be spotted by their repeated references to Isaiah 53:5 and 1 Peter 2:24: 'By his stripes you were healed,' is their cry when they are talking and praying about healing. They tend to imply that all believers should experience all the benefits of the cross immediately, and so do not sufficiently acknowledge the glorious transformation which is to come. They do look with great hope to the day of resurrection, but they consider that all God's healing promises are fully for this life. This means that, for some, they have a false level of hope for healing in the present.

This approach rightly stresses that Jesus fully and finally dealt with all our sickness on the cross, but it goes on to suggest that we can claim our healing by faith in much the same way that we can claim our forgiveness by faith. Passages like James 5:14–15 and Matthew 9:1–7 do show that forgiveness and healing are closely connected, but it surely is a mistake to equate them directly.

Forgiveness is the primary blessing of salvation – it is the greatest miracle of all and God's priority for our lives – whereas healing is only part of God's full salvation. The New Testament focus is always on forgiveness in and by Christ; healing is merely a sign which points to something much greater. We saw this in many of the Old Testament miracles, and we can see it, for example, in Matthew 9:1–7, where the healing miracle occurs 'that you may know the Son of Man has power on earth to forgive sins'.

Divine forgiveness is the most fundamental and basic eternal necessity for all humanity. We are doomed without it and it is freely available in Christ, through the cross, to those who believe and trust in him. Divine healing is associated with forgiveness. It is a part of salvation which is available now for all forgiven believers and will be completed at the last day. However, healing is also a wonderful gift which God, in his gracious compassion, also gives to many unbelievers as a sign pointing them towards his forgiveness.

Even if it were right to equate healing with forgiveness, we would still have to recognise that there is an important element of forgiveness and justification which will not be experienced until the day of resurrection. No matter how great our faith, or how full our experience of God's saving grace in this life, there will still be even more for us to look forward to at the final day when we stand before God.

It is the same with healing. A saint who experienced by faith the fullest possible degree of divine forgiveness, and lived continually in Christ's complete victory over sin, would not be immune to accidents or viruses, and would age, deteriorate and die. Romans 8 expounds the wonderful truth that we have been set free from the law of sin and death, but it also explains that those who have the firstfruits of the Spirit are still part of the groaning creation which is waiting for the redemption of the body.

Believers in this healing tradition are right in their belief that Christ's redeeming death guarantees healing. They are wrong, however, when they assert that the benefits of his death can and should be experienced fully and completely now. Paul makes it clear in Romans 8 that we were saved in hope, but that hope which is seen is not hope. This means that there must be an unseen, unexperienced element to our salvation and Christian experience – that there is something for God to complete at the last day. Paul urges us to hope for what we do not see and to eagerly wait for it with perseverance, whereas many leaders in this tradition accuse us of lacking faith if we do not fully experience the benefits of the cross right now.

Some proponents of the atonement emphasis suggest that forgiveness and healing are benefits which are fully available now by faith, but that resurrection and redemption are benefits which are reserved for the future. While it is true that some things are available to us now and that we must wait for other things at the resurrection, we must be careful that we do not make a false distinction between forgiveness and redemption of the body, and between healing and resurrection. Physical redemption and resurrection are not something radically new and different, they are the fulfilment – or completion – of forgiveness and healing. In fact, it should be plain that there would be no need for resurrection or physical redemption if we experienced full and complete forgiveness and healing on earth.

God's work of redemption is not 'pie in the sky when we die' or 'pie before we die'; nor is it two different pies, one for complete consumption 'now' and a different one which is reserved for 'then'. Instead, there is just one huge redemption pie, and we take the largest bite that we can manage at conversion, and can go on munching right through our earthly life. But, no matter how great our appetite, there is always far more of the same single pie left for the last day – when we will get the lot, all in one go!

Paul was miraculously healed on at least two occasions, and he was often God's partner in ministering physical healing to others. Nobody can accuse him of not believing that healing was for the present. But he knew that there were greater things in store at the resurrection which he should hope for, eagerly expect, and wait for with perseverance. Just as the sovereignty emphasis is mistaken in looking for divine healing mainly in the future, so the atonement emphasis is unbalanced in exaggerating our experience of miraculous healing in the present. As with so many aspects of Christianity, the truth is 'both' – not 'either or'.

There is much that is good in the atonement tradition, for it can never be wrong to place the cross at the centre of any aspect of the Christian life, and it is very helpful to keep on being reminded about the link between healing and the redemptive work of Christ. In particular, its emphasis on Isaiah 53:4–5 is very important.

This approach rightly points to Matthew 8:14–17 as clear proof that Jesus' healing ministry is the fulfilment of Isaiah 53:4–5, and reminds us that Jesus came to relieve us of the burdens of sin and sickness, that his wounds really do make us whole. But critics of this emphasis suggest that it misses part of the significance of Matthew 8:17.

Isaiah 53 is a prophecy that the bearing of sickness and pain will take place on the cross, yet Matthew 8 claims that Jesus' pre-Calvary ministry is the fulfilment of Isaiah's prophecy. We can understand the important point that Jesus healed and forgave people in advance of the cross in two complementary ways. First, we can appreciate that Jesus did this on the basis of what he was to do on the cross. It should not surprise us that he was able to heal people before he paid the price for sickness and sin, as he was dealing with humanity in blessing – especially Israel – thousands of years before the cross. They got it on credit! And, second, we can think of Jesus' earthly healing ministry as a function – or foreshadowing – of his substitutionary death. The way that he dealt with sickness in his life paved the way for his destruction of death and sickness on the cross.

Isaiah 53 makes it impossible for us to separate healing from the cross. It shows that by bearing our sin and iniquity Jesus bore our sickness and pain; that by taking our guilt he incurred our punishment; and that total healing has come at the cost of his wounds. The whole person has been wholly healed. The sick nation has been fully restored and made well.

89

In the land of the majestic king, foreseen in Isaiah 33:17–24, the inhabitants will not say, 'I am sick,' because they 'will be forgiven their iniquity'. If we take the Bible seriously, we must agree that this approach to healing is correct in its claim that sickness is banished because sin has been vanquished.

This tradition also helpfully emphasises the need for faith or belief in the person seeking healing, but – sadly – it gives the dangerous false impression that the corollary is also true. However, a lack of healing is not inevitably due to the presence of sin or the absence of faith in the person feeling sick.

We have seen that there are passages where Jesus states that a particular lack of healing can be explained by the absence of faith in either the minister or those needing ministry. But it is ludicrous to suggest, for example, that the lame man at the pool of Bethesda was healed because he had faith and that all the sick people around him were not healed because they lacked faith. The long and painful story of Job shows us just how wrong and hurtful it is to suggest that a lack of healing is inevitably due to the sick person's sin or lack of faith. At times, some of the modern believers who are nurtured within this healing tradition seem to be no more than the modern counterparts of Eliphaz, Bildad and Zophar!

Faith and holiness are important factors in divine healing, but they are not the only ones. This healing emphasis is flawed because it often ignores the sovereignty of God, overlooks our partnership with God, and neglects the anointing with the Spirit. Concentrating as it does on the healing of believers, it has little to say about evangelism; and – due to its characteristic emphasis on health and wealth – it has even less to say about living in a way which facilitates reaching the poor. I recognise that some leaders within this tradition are passionately committed both to evangelism and ministry to the poor, but the picture I have painted of the general atonement approach is accurate.

The cross must be part of our understanding of healing – and it is undoubtedly a major aspect of the *why* of contemporary divine healing. But the healing ideas associated with the atonement emphasis must be tempered by the other two traditions.

*A* third approach to healing focuses more on the Holy Spirit, and stresses the anointing or the enabling of the Spirit upon the believer who is ministering the healing. Believers from this tradition can usually be recognised by their frequent use of phrases like 'power ministry' and 'special anointing', and they look to verses like Luke 5:17, John 5:8 and Acts 5:12–16 to justify these ideas.

This approach correctly emphasises the idea of our fellowship or partnership with God, and the need for both the anointing with the Holy Spirit and the Spirit's prompting to release and direct God's power. It rightly encourages all believers to pray and to get involved in Christ's ministry, and urges us to see that God wants to work with and through all his disciples. But despite this helpful emphasis on 'every member ministry', there is a tendency within the tradition to forget the 'novice Ananias' principle and focus on a few special ministers of healing.

This tradition tends to see everything in terms of the Spirit's anointing. Whenever anyone is healed – no matter how minor the ailment or slight the improvement – the event is identified as a miracle and explained as the work of the Holy Spirit. Even if the person healed has been medically treated and lovingly cared for, the cure is always ascribed only to the Spirit – no other factors are acknowledged, whatever has gone before is forgotten.

On its own this emphasis says little about God's sovereignty, and even less about Christ's atonement. Its understanding of healing is based essentially in the gospel stories, and the wider biblical teaching about sickness and the cross is usually not proclaimed. Whenever a gospel story is studied, this tradition looks closely at Jesus the healer and neglects the person receiving healing. It concentrates on suggesting that we can and should minister with the same frequency and the same effectiveness as Jesus because we have the same Spirit. Yet it seems to ignore the factors of Jesus' divinity, his sinlessness, his perfect obedience and the important point that he received the Spirit 'without measure'. This tradition does proclaim the role of healing as a sign confirming the word in evangelism, but – in practice – this is usually a peripheral matter left to a few specialist ministers.

Despite all the claims, most ordinary believers nurtured within this tradition minister only to other believers about minor matters in meetings. Few expect to see a lame beggar walk or a deaf atheist hear through their personal ministry. They might hope to heal the occasional headache of someone in their housegroup, but they would take someone who was seriously ill along to a meeting to be prayed for by a famous minister. This common attitude often leads to the false idea that a particular man or woman is a spiritual healer with a spiritual healing ministry, when the truth is that God is the only healer and the most we can have is a small share in Christ's ministry.

Although the Spirit is given to floodlight – to focus attention on – the eternal God, this healing emphasis often concentrates on 'me and my ministry' in the present. This has led, at times, to its becoming a rather introspective tradition which is not concerned with the final, future, perfect healing. There is a reasoned and realistic hope for healing for today within this tradition, but many are too busy praying for more power for themselves to relax in the hope of God's promise of transformation at the day of resurrection.

In this anointing emphasis, a lack of healing is often blamed on insufficient faith or too much sin in the life of the person ministering, or on not enough prayer or fasting, or on poor ministry techniques. The focus is all on the believer ministering and an absence of healing is rarely understood in terms of God's sovereignty. This means that the presence of healing is often accredited to the faith and saintliness of the minister rather than to the power and grace of God, hence the considerable devotion and acclaim given to those men and women who are considered to have special ministries of healing.

The gifts of the Spirit – especially the word of knowledge – are frequently and helpfully used in this healing tradition, and comforting physical phenomena are commonly associated with anointed healing ministries. These phenomena – falling, shaking, resting, tingling, laughing, weeping, and so on – are sometimes sought for their own sake and are often misunderstood as a measure of healing power rather than as a natural bodily reaction to God's presence.

Often too much attention is placed on special healing techniques. It is almost as though the very mechanics of the way we pray for healing, or the special atmosphere of a meeting, determine whether or not the person is healed!

The fashion in healing ministry seems to vary from group to group. Some people lightly touch the sick person with their right hand and stretch their left hand up to God; others vibrate both hands about six inches away from the sick person; some insist on placing both their hands firmly on the person's head; a few never touch the individual they are praying for because they are worried that they might be affected by a demonic influence. Some believers pray with their eyes wide open, others with their eyes tightly shut. There are leaders who shout commands, others who whisper requests, those who repeat the same phrase several times, and a few who blow into microphones.

Some disciples nurtured in this tradition foolishly think that they will start healing people as soon as they exactly duplicate the precise ministry action of their favourite anointed leader. When this happens, it is little wonder that critics accuse the healing ministry of too much fleshly self-effort.

We could say that the sovereignty emphasis concentrates on God and says there is no healing without his will; that the atonement emphasis looks at the person being healed and asserts there is no healing without faith; and that the anointing emphasis centres on the believer ministering and maintains there is no healing without an empowering by the Spirit. All these emphases are right, but not to the exclusion of the others. Each has something important to teach us about healing. And it should be obvious that we need to hold the best aspects of them together in the same sort of balance we see in the Trinity.

We need to recognise, acknowledge and make room for God's sovereignty – even when we cannot fully understand it! The anointing of the Spirit upon Peter and John may explain *how* the lame man was healed in Acts 3, but God's sovereignty is surely the only answer to questions about *why* this particular man was healed on that specific day. We can debate whether the primary means for the cure of the lame man in John 5 was Jesus' divine authority or his prophetic anointing, but God's sovereignty is the only possible explanation for the man's isolated cure and the continued sickness of all the other people around him. It would be nice to think that the extraordinary events at Nyota Farm were due to my saintliness, but I know that it was God's season for special blessing.

In 1993, on a trip to Brazil, I was ministering at a conference in São Paulo when a sick man's teeth were sovereignly transformed – his mouth was instantly filled with what appeared to be gold fillings. I visited Brazil twice that year, and each time saw God work a succession of dental miracles. I even met one lady who found that her mouth had been suddenly filled with thirteen gold inlays in her teeth; and a local non-Christian dentist who attended one meeting to challenge the claims was himself given a new tooth!

One of the meetings was broadcast live on radio. A woman listening in São Paulo, who was too poor to visit a dentist, found her mouth suddenly filled with what seemed to be brand new teeth. I examined her later and her teeth glistened. They were incredibly well formed – quite unlike the teeth of all the hundreds of thousands of people living around her in poverty with no dental or medical care.

I was so puzzled by these miracles that I took my own British dentist with me to Brazil to check that what had been happening was real. She examined twelve dental miracles and made a series of observations.

1. There was no dental reason why some teeth had gold fillings and others did not.

2. The price of the dental work was too great for the people to have been able to pay for it.

3. The quality of work was outstanding – she described it as 'perfection'.

4. She suspected that regular dentistry work was being transformed into divine dentistry – that existing poor fillings were being changed into perfect ones.

5. She had never before seen the kind of gold-based

amalgam in the 'miracle' teeth in human dental work.

I can only explain isolated incidents like these in terms of God's sovereignty. We will offer little hope, however, to the great mass of hurting people if we focus too much on God's sovereignty and fail to grasp that he is filled with an incredible general willingness to heal. If we over-emphasise his sovereignty, we can appear to suggest that he is a reluctant and begrudging healer rather than the greatest and most generous physician of all.

We need to remember that the 'atonement' is the clearest possible expression of God's sovereign will, and that the cross has made complete and perfect healing possible for all creation. The wonderful truth is that Christ's death shows healing for all and this is God's perfect sovereign will. In this earthly life, however, other matters are sometimes more urgent and central to his purposes for our lives. Perhaps we should start to think about God's sovereignty more as the answer to puzzles about a lack of healing rather than as the main explanation for an occurrence of healing.

Any and every issue of healing should bring us back to God. Whenever we see or experience healing, we should go to him with praise and rejoicing because he is the ultimate source of all genuine healing. Equally, whenever we are struggling with a lack of apparent healing, we should turn to him for comfort, strength and fresh revelation of his purposes. Either way, we should always thank him for his promise, in the cross, of ultimate healing, and should go on asking him to increase our hope and our eager expectation of that perfect healing which is to come.

# 10

# A TRINITARIAN APPROACH

W hen evangelical and Pentecostal believers speak about God, they tend to concentrate on the redemptive side of God's nature, whereas both the Old and the New Testaments celebrate him equally as Creator and as Redeemer. If we are to become truly biblical in our thinking and worship, we need to appreciate, adore and proclaim both sides of the divine character. This is especially true in healing where we need to grasp that God heals people both because he is the Creator and also because he is the Redeemer.

We can look for – and find – explanations for healing in both the creative and the redemptive sides of God's nature, so we need to point people to both aspects of his healing, to show that there is no contradiction or competition between them, and to encourage people to embrace both as complementary – neither redemptive nor creative healing is better or superior than the other.

A s Creator, God has implanted a self-healing principle into his creation. Whenever we cut ourselves or catch a disease, God uses the natural processes he designed to begin the process of healing. Our bodies have been programmed by him to resist disease and to recover from cuts and bruises. Of course, there are many diseases and accidents from which we cannot fully recover, but all creation has been given some capacity for healing. Sometimes God considerably speeds up this natural process – Christians often call this a miracle – while, at other times, he slows the natural healing process down because he wants to draw attention to some other aspect of our lives.

God also uses those natural medical remedies which humanity has 'discovered' and developed from within God's creation. Again, the Creator often intervenes – either sovereignly or in answer to prayer – and surprises medical staff by dramatically speeding up the medical healing processes. Of course, we can all resist Creator God and not co-operate with him by refusing to rest or by rejecting his principles of diet, fitness, hygiene and health.

Several of the miraculous healings experienced by our members involve speedier recoveries than expected by medical experts. For example, one of our girls fell down a flight of stairs at Hamburg station while travelling to Russia to take part in an evangelistic mission. She was taken to a local hospital where X-rays revealed that her arm was badly broken. It was put in plaster and she was told that the cast must not come off for at least eight weeks. Because of the mission, there was much prayer for a quick healing and within two weeks the same doctors declared that 'a miracle has taken place'. The bones in her arm had mended perfectly and she was completely healed.

This was not an 'instant' supernatural miracle like the Brazilian gold teeth or the restoration of the severed ear in Gethsemane. Rather, it was an extraordinary divine 'speeding up' of the natural healing process, suitably assisted by medical treatment and sensible rest.

In another case, a member gave birth prematurely to twins. Sadly, one was stillborn and the other weighed only 2 lbs. The staff said that the living baby had a problem with her spleen, her liver and her heart, and was unlikely to survive. Another member was also in the special care unit with a premature baby, and we united in praying for the two families and their children.

After nearly two months, the surviving twin had to have open heart surgery. The operation lasted over four hours, but the baby's recovery was then incredibly quick. Within a few hours of the operation she was well enough to leave intensive care and enter the ward; four days later she was strong enough to go home. The doctors were amazed and said that they could not understand how she had recovered so quickly without even the slightest setback.

Again, this was not an 'instant and complete' miracle, instead, God seems to have been deeply involved 'lubricating' the medical process and hastening recovery by his power. I suspect that few non-Christian people would call this a 'miracle', but they would be just as thrilled as we were by the wonderful recovery. We thanked the staff *and* praised God.

As Redeemer, God has eternally dealt with sin and death in Christ on the cross, and, therefore, he has dealt with all the consequences of sin – including sickness. The price Christ paid with his blood for our redemption unconditionally guarantees that all believers can look forward with absolute certainty to a resurrected, reconstructed, perfect body and to a pain-free, tear-free, eternal existence in the personal presence of God. At the last day, because of Calvary, all true believers will be totally transformed: every healing they experienced in this life will be completed and fulfilled; every weakness, disability and impediment will be instantly changed into a glorious and radiant perfection. This is the wonder towards which all earthly healing points.

This is so wonderful that we must ensure that the cross is central in everything we do and preach. The cross – and the rejection of Christ that led to it – is the worst possible event that could ever happen, yet it is God's precious act of salvation for the whole world. On the cross, Jesus paid the full price for all sin, sickness, pain and death – it really is true that by his stripes we are healed. But we are doomed to despair and disappointment if we think this means that sickness will not trouble us in this life, or that we have an automatic right to immediate and complete healing today.

We believe that Jesus dealt with death on the cross, but we know that we still have to die physically. His victory over death gives us wonderful hope for the future and enables us to face the present process of dying with peace and equanimity.

We also know that Jesus dealt with every type of sin on the cross, but this does not mean that we are fully immune from all the contemporary effects of sin. His triumph over sin provides us with glorious hope for a joyous, stress-free eternal life – and it also helps us to endure with patience all the tribulations of our earthly life.

As we have seen, the cross does not guarantee us automatic physical healing in this life – even if we are fully obedient and full of faith. We offer hurting people false hope when we concentrate entirely on one aspect of redemption and ignore the other factors involved in healing. Equally, we offer hurting believers false no-hope if we reject the truth that we can experience a foretaste of the eternal healing here and now.

Many of our members – especially the Africans – have been nurtured in the atonement approach to healing, and they are very hot on claiming their healing by faith in the stripes of Jesus. Time and again they are not disappointed. One member had suffered for years from piles with bleeding and excruciating pain. One Sunday afternoon in 1996, when the bleeding was particularly severe, he decided that it was time for him to receive his healing. He asked God to confirm the healing in some way at our morning service, and took comfort in a reference to being healed by the blood. He went home and started claiming every biblical promise that he could find about healing: within two weeks his piles were perfectly and permanently healed.

Similarly, back in 1990, a member gave birth in hospital to a stillborn child. Two days after being discharged, the woman – who was herself a midwife – began to bleed. She was prescribed the appropriate drugs, but they had no effect; four weeks after the birth she was still bleeding copiously. The hospital were so concerned that they decided to operate. The husband was worried that his wife would die during the operation, so on the evening before the operation they visited our weekly healing clinic for prayer and advice.

After prayer, they decided that they should claim their healing by faith, and ask God to stop the bleeding without an operation. They prayed and prayed that night, but the bleeding continued. During the night, however, the woman dreamt that the Lord was telling her she was healed. When she woke, the bleeding really had stopped and she rang the hospital to cancel the operation. The staff only believed her because she was one of their midwives.

Most testimonies about healing through the atonement are not so dramatic. Even so, many of our members consider that prayer is a much more effective painkiller than paracetamol. This is a typical testimony: 'About a couple of months ago, I had a terrible pain in my abdominal area. I confessed the healing power of Jesus and asked my nineteen-year-old son to pray for me. He laid his hand on my abdomen and prayed in the name of Jesus. The pain miraculously disappeared and has never returned to this day. Praise God!'

In the last thirty years, the liberating truths about living with the Spirit and ministering with his power have transformed vast sections of the Church throughout the world. Believers have started to understand that God wants to use them in ministry, as well as using those in full-time service, and the healing ministry has mushroomed. Groups have been started to intercede for healing, to pray with those needing healing, and to pray for those involved in medical care and medical healing. Special times of healing ministry have been developed during services and a general atmosphere of hopeful healing expectancy has developed. This has all been good, right and helpful.

At Kensington Temple, we have trained many of our members to lead a weekly healing clinic and when necessary to participate as a healing team in our meetings. I sometimes issue general invitations for sick people to come forward for prayer during our services, and it is our trained members who minister to them. This ensures that there is not too great an emphasis on ministry by one particular individual at the front. I am also always alert for the Spirit's prompting that God wants to heal a particular person.

Those of us who are leading the services at Kensington Temple are free to minister under the Spirit's anointing. When we sense the Spirit's prompting, we announce what we understand to be his words. A while ago on a Sunday morning, I felt led to say that God was going to heal someone who had had a series of three operations in exactly the same place. A lady stood up and said that she had had three operations on her right big toe, and was suffering from acute rejection of an artificial joint in the toe. She was instantly healed and has not needed a further operation. The toe immediately began functioning properly for the first time and she was released from a continuous fear of being knocked on the toe, a fear which had restricted her activities.

At another meeting on a Friday night, I felt sure the Spirit was telling me that someone with a long-standing bowel complaint was going to be healed. A lady indicated that she had such a problem and we prayed for her – however, I sensed somehow that the Spirit really meant someone with a much more serious condition.

Another lady was present in the meeting who had been ill for twenty-seven years with a terrible bowel condition which needed considerable medication – she had to take a dozen tablets every night. This lady, who was a nurse, had also damaged her back lifting some heavy equipment and had to wear a steel corset all the time. She was too shy to respond publicly to my words, but – while we were praying for the other lady – she felt the power of God come upon her and cure the bowel complaint. When she got home, she found to her amazement that God had also healed her back: she has been free from pain ever since and has not needed any medication or support.

I recognise, however, that there are possible dangers in this approach. If there is too great a focus on the person ministering at the front, there is bound to be too little attention on God. And if there is too much stress on the Spirit, we will miss the main purpose of his activity, which is to make Jesus better known.

We must remember that the cross, not the dove, is the great symbol of our faith, and must develop an understanding of healing which focuses on Christ – not on the Spirit, and definitely not on the man or woman at the front – and which also fully embraces those aspects of healing which are rooted in the creative side of God's nature.

If we are to develop a full and mature grasp of divine healing, I believe that we must learn to hold the Father's sovereignty, the Son's atonement and the Spirit's anointing in close harmony.

This more complete understanding of the principles involved in divine healing will equip us to answer the difficult questions posed by a cynical society and to minister in a way which brings genuine, realistic hope to the hurting people around us.

Viewed from one angle, God the Father is far away – a transcendental interferer who breaks into a hurting world to heal supernaturally only when he chooses, whom he chooses and how he chooses. Yet, viewed another way, he is also close by – an immanent lover who has filled his groaning creation with a tremendous variety of means to satisfy its deep yearning for healing. The wonderful truth is that the Father is full of an overwhelming willingness to heal which he perfectly reveals immanently in creation, in Christ, on the cross, and through the Spirit – and transcendentally through sovereign miracles.

God the Son is the great physician who came to bind up the broken-hearted, to liberate the captives and to give sight to the blind. In the power of his name and under the anointing of the Spirit, he healed many in Israel. Then, on the cross, through the sacrifice of his blood, he purchased the absolute healing of all people – present, past and future. The risen Son charged his followers with continuing his healing, saving ministry throughout the world – but made it clear that they needed the anointing and enabling of the Spirit in order to share in his ministry. We can say that the Spirit's anointing enables us to apply to others – and to experience for ourselves – the healing that the Father has willed and the Son has achieved.

This integration in healing between the anointing and the atonement can often be seen at work. A lady called Marian was diagnosed with very high blood pressure, and she began praying every day for her healing by claiming the atonement promises. Several months later, at a Friday evening meeting, I sensed that the Spirit was urging me to say that someone called Marian was going to be healed. When I announced this, nobody called Marian was present at the meeting. However, one of Marian's close friends was there, and she was so excited that she visited Marian straight after the meeting to pass on God's message.

Marian was tremendously encouraged, but she was not

instantly healed. She soon noticed, however, that the pressure had begun to fall. She carried on claiming her healing through the stripes of Christ and her blood pressure was back to normal within a couple of months – and has not troubled her since. I knew nothing about all this until she sent me her testimony when I was writing this book.

When I first began to minister in this way with the Spirit, I assumed that incidents like this were probably spiritual mistakes on my part. If nobody responded publicly to the 'word' in the meeting I felt rather condemned and foolish. But so many reports of healing have come back months after the 'word of knowledge' that I am now more confident in God's work. I have come to realise that his priority is healing people, not publicising me as a good servant!

The Father's sovereignty, the Son's atonement and the Spirit's anointing are the three basic principles which lie behind all supernatural divine healing, and we will have an unbalanced understanding if we over-emphasise one or overlook another. Many leaders present the atonement and the anointing as a healing paradox which needs to be held in tension – rather like God's sovereignty and humanity's free will. But a trinitarian understanding of healing enables us to integrate the three principles and weave them together into a satisfying and accurate understanding which is based in the eternal work of God.

There are many ways of considering this. At creation, we see the Father willing, the Word speaking and the Spirit enacting. We see the same pattern in the healings before Calvary – the Father willed, the Word spoke to and directed God's servants the prophets, and the Spirit empowered and enabled them. It is hardly any different with the healings after Calvary – the Father's will and willingness to heal are visible in the atonement; the Son has acted to purchase healing through the atonement, and he directs his servants where and how to apply it; and the Spirit still empowers and enables us.

We can also see the integration of the principles when we think about healing as part of our personal experience of salvation. It was the Father's good will that eternal life should be won for us – and given freely to us – by Christ on the cross; and his gift of the Spirit to us is the seal or guarantee of our eternal existence. Our anointing in and with the Holy Spirit is the firstfruit, or the foreshadowing, of the inheritance which God has chosen for us in Christ. Healing is one aspect of that inheritance, so we have a tangible foretaste now – in and through the Spirit – of the perfect healing to come.

We can also appreciate this trinitarian integration by considering healing as part of the Church's commissioning. In Matthew 28:16–20, the resurrected Jesus charges his disciples to go to all nations and make disciples. He refers to the Father, the Son and the Spirit, and promises to be with us to the end of the age. In Mark 16:15–20, Jesus tells his disciples to go and preach the gospel – the good news of the cross – to all creatures. He lists healing as a special sign which validates the gospel message and points to the redeeming God. Here, the Son works with us and confirms our message with miraculous signs. In Luke 24:44–49, Jesus roots everything in the Scriptures. He highlights the cross and the world-wide preaching of the gospel, and urges his disciples to wait until they are endued with power from on high. Here, the Son pledges to send the Father's promise – which is the Spirit. And in John 20:21–23, Jesus commissions his disciples to go 'As the Father has sent me,' and says, 'Receive the Holy Spirit.'

There is a thoroughly trinitarian understanding of mission in these passages which incorporates the Son's atonement, the Father's will and the Spirit's anointing. We have been sent by the Son – in the same way that he was sent by the Father – to preach the message of the cross, to make disciples of the cross, to bear witness to the crucified, risen Lord, and to reconcile sinners to the Father. But we can only do this effectively if we have been anointed with the Spirit. It is through the Spirit that Jesus accompanies us, works with us, and provides signs – healing miracles – which confirm the message of the cross, point to him and direct people back to the welcoming Father.

We are unlikely to fall into error or an unbalanced emphasis when our understanding of healing is deeply rooted in this way in the nature of the triune God. His great willingness to heal – at the cross, in the present and at the last day – should

be more than enough to cause us to live with enormous h[e]
for healing, and to be ready to be deeply involved in taki[ng]
his healing to the hurting people around us.

*A*s well as integrating the basic principles of divine healing
in a trinitarian way, we should also try to maintain a
balance of emphasis between the faith involved in the healing,
the anointing of the believer who is ministering, and the sovereignty of God.

In any instance of healing or failure to heal, one of these
factors will always seem more evident, and there will be
occasional times when one or more appears to be absent.
However, the truth is that they are always deeply integrated.
None of them is always the main reason for the absence or
presence of healing – they are all involved in some way.

For example, God's sovereignty is the overarching, super-
intending influence which does not only determine that healing
occurs, but also the how, where and when! Equally, there will
usually be faith somewhere – whether in the person healed,
the believer ministering, or in friends and relatives who have
gone on praying for many years. We might not see the faith,
but I guarantee that it will almost always be there somewhere.

It is much the same with questions about sickness: there is
no one simple explanation which answers every inquiry
correctly. Religious people are always wanting to know *why*
someone is ill; for example, the disciples in John 9 wanted to
know whether a man was blind because he or his parents had
sinned. Jesus showed them that their personal sin had nothing
to do with it, and in Luke 13:1–5 we read that he rejected the
idea that people were maimed and killed in an accident because
they had sinned.

The Scriptures are more interested in emphasising God's
willingness to heal than in examining the causes of sickness,
in celebrating Christ's victory rather than crowing about Satan's
defeat. We must remember that we have been called not to
define the devil, but to resist him; not to describe him, but to
renounce him. We have been commissioned to trample Satan
and all his works under our feet, not to study his squashed
corpse through a magnifying glass. However, the issue of

sickness does trouble many believers. They want to know where it comes from, and how its existence is compatible with an all-powerful, omnipresent, all-loving God.

We need to examine this issue in a little more detail and try to unravel some of the scriptural ideas and responses – while never forgetting that our focus must always be fixed on the all-healing God.

# Part Three

# LOOKING AT HEALING ISSUES

# 11

# SICKNESS AND SIN

$A$ cts 10:38 is an important verse for us as it contains the first summary of the gospel given to Gentiles. Peter, prompted by the Spirit to enter a non-Jewish home for the first time in his life, and speaking under the influence of the Holy Spirit, introduced Jesus to Cornelius' household and explained what 'the word' was which had been proclaimed. 'God anointed Jesus of Nazareth with the Holy Spirit and with power, who went about doing good and healing all who were oppressed by the devil, for God was with him.'

Peter's summary demonstrates that healing anointing is the heart of the gospel and mission. It is about power, doing good, and partnering with God. Acts 10:38 also shows us that healing is not just about eliminating disease and disorder: healing also means dealing with the devil.

Some believers simplistically insist that each disease and every disaster is due to a single cause, though they may differ among themselves as to the cause. Many of us are as blinkered in our thinking about sickness as we are in our ideas about healing. Acts 10:38 shows us that we cannot ignore the devil when we are considering these issues.

Just as we need to establish a trinitarian approach to healing which weaves together the best aspects of the different emphases, so we need to develop a more integrated understanding of sickness. Somehow we need to hold together three basic spiritual facts about sickness. First, that all sickness is intrinsically evil and a consequence of the fall; second, that in redeeming us from sin, Christ paid the full price for sickness on the cross; and, third, that all believers are part of God's groaning creation which is waiting for the redemption of the body – and, therefore, are still subject to sickness.

When medical specialists seek to help someone who is ill, they want to know *what* the precise sickness is which is afflicting the person. Effective medical treatment depends on a prompt and accurate diagnosis of the ailment or disease. Once the doctors have discovered exactly what is wrong, they can prescribe the appropriate drug and suggest the best course of treatment. Experience, education and training are paramount; without them there is little hope for a medical cure from sickness.

But Christian ministers seeking to help a sick person are more concerned with *why* the person is ill and *how* God wants them to proceed. Divine healing depends on a good understanding of the causes behind the condition, not on an accurate identification of the sickness. Even then, the divine cure for sickness will vary from person to person irrespective of the condition or the cause.

The prescribed spiritual treatment for leprosy, for example, is not repeated bathing in the River Jordan – that was only God's way for Naaman. Equally, the Christian cure for blindness does not always involve the application of a saliva and soil paste to the eyes – that was Jesus' way with one man. And the Spirit's patent remedy for every upset stomach is not a glass of wine – though it was for Timothy. Listening to the Spirit, recognising his direction, and obeying his promptings are critical in divine healing, which is why a novice like Ananias can be just as effective a healing partner as the most experienced minister.

We will look at these two fundamentally different approaches in the next two chapters when we consider the issues of medical verification and the criteria for miracles. However, we need to appreciate now that many of the criticisms of the Christian healing ministry are due to a failure to appreciate the importance of the difference between a medical and a spiritual approach to sickness.

It should be obvious that people become ill for a wide variety of reasons. Some are sick because God has allowed the evil one to use weakness and disease to test them – as with Job. It would be as much a waste of time for an anointed believer to pray for Job's boils to go away as it would be for a doctor to try to treat them medically.

Other people are ill because they have ignored God's principles of diet, fitness, hygiene and a healthy lifestyle. Christians who eat too much and exercise too little are just as prone to heart disease as their unbelieving neighbours. Prayer and drugs might help them when they become seriously ill, but most overweight believers should think again about the way they are misusing God's gifts, and seek help to change the way that they live before their useful service is curtailed.

Still more men and women become sick because they are innocent victims of the corporate sin, greed, selfishness and stress of our fallen society – pollution and war, for example, do not discriminate between the just and unjust. When people are injured or ill in this way, they need urgent medical help *and* persistent prayer. Our brothers and sisters overseas who are caught up in poverty and conflict do need our prayers, but they desperately need medical help – and our finance to provide it. At times, prayer for healing can be a sinful excuse for inaction.

A few people – like the saints in 1 Corinthians 11:27–34 – may be ill because God is using a form of sickness to chasten them. In other cases, one or two might be disabled so that the glory of God can be revealed through their healing – as in John 9:1–3. And some, like Trophimus, are just sick – we don't know why, we can't know why, we simply have to encourage them to rest, to care for them, and to go on praying for them without resigning them to their sickness.

We can see from these simple illustrations that there are many causes of sickness, so we need insight from God to understand what his remedy is in each case. Not everyone needs to have an evil spirit cast out to be healed – but, occasionally, one might. Not all people need to repent of a deep sin before they can be healed – but some do. Not everybody needs to be immediately directed to a medical expert – but many do. Not all sick people need to be encouraged to ask God for patience and strength to endure the illness – but some do need his help to endure hardship without losing any hope for his healing. I

111

cannot overstate how important it is that we listen carefully to God's Spirit and do not rely merely on our own experience and inclination. We should not rule out basic common sense, and we do need to follow biblical principles, but we must pay close attention to the promptings of the Holy Spirit.

One of the most common Christian attitudes to sickness is to think that it is all due to the devil. Whenever someone is ill in a church, there is always a group of believers who will insist that we must start rebuking Satan loudly and blame him for the illness. Equally, there is always another group who will glory in the sickness and maintain that it is God's wonderful way of blessing and refining us.

Both of these attitudes have some truth in them, and each may be right in particular instances. But we should move beyond such superficial ideas and establish some scriptural principles about sickness which ensure that we do not drift into an unhelpful extremism.

The most basic biblical principle of all is that God is good, and – by definition – a good God does not impose any form of evil on anyone: verses like James 1:17, 1 John 1:5 and Genesis 1:31 illustrate this widely understood principle. This means that our Christian understanding of sickness should be founded on the insistence that no form of sickness can ever have its source in God. He is not the creator of disease, sickness or death. These things were never part of God's original plan for humanity.

Creation was made perfect by God and was not tainted in any way by disease or death. All living creatures were made without sickness, and humanity was formed in the image of the life-giving, all-loving Creator – which must mean that the first man and woman were completely free from sickness.

If sickness was not originally part of God's creation, it is an obvious question to ask where it came from. In the Bible, the answer is shrouded in the same mystery as the origin of evil itself. I believe the most we can say with certainty is that sickness came into the world through sin.

Some believers maintain that every sickness comes directly from the devil, but I think that is rather too simplistic. Of course, Satan uses sickness – much as he uses death – but the Bible does not ascribe to him the creative power needed to form disease. He is not almighty, and was originally made by God himself. He may have become 'Satan' – the adversary – but he is not God's equal and he is not eternal. Sickness may be one of the weapons he uses, but we must be careful not to confuse his use of sickness with the idea that he has the power or capacity to create sickness.

The evil one existed as Lucifer long before sin came into the world. Isaiah 14 and Ezekiel 28 move from describing contemporary human rulers into offering prophetic, parabolic insights into the ejection of the evil one from heaven. The five-fold 'I will' in Isaiah 14:13–14 shows that naked, selfish ambition was the very first evil to pollute God's free creation. It seems that Lucifer was dissatisfied with his position below God and wanted to usurp him; he was ambitious to become God and tried to depose him – that is why he fell.

These two passages suggest that evil emerged from Lucifer's ambitious assertion of self-will against God's will, from a desire to dominate and control. Thus sin came into being – it is perhaps better to say that it emerged rather than that it was made. All the consequences of sin, including sickness, stem from this initial ambition and rebellion.

The cause of Lucifer's fall then became his principal weapon in the war that he has waged ever since against God and his creation. Every form of sin is rooted and shaped in his ambitious self-will. Every disease and sickness – from the mildest cold to the most hideous cancer – is a direct consequence of this, and is part of Lucifer's cosmic struggle to dominate, control, corrupt and destroy God's perfect order. Of course, he cannot win, as God is sovereign and over all, but Satan can cause considerable harm and mayhem until God brings his rebellion to an end.

When we think dispassionately about sickness, we can see that every type is merely a different expression of an ambitious desire to impose control and corruption on every part of creation. Even death itself – the ultimate fruit of sin – is only the complete domination and corruption of one part of creation by evil. Every aspect of sin – whether personal, corporate, or that which is inherent in a fallen world – bears the image of the original sin.

*O*ur understanding of sickness is incomplete, however, if we think about it only in terms of the devil and his work. We also need to appreciate that sickness is an element both of 'the curse' which God put upon the world because of humanity's fall, and of 'the curse of the law' which God put on his people because of their disobedience.

The Bible reveals that Yahweh Rapha, the healing God of Israel, delights to bless as far as the thousandth generation. But it also makes it clear that he will curse to the third generation when there is a just cause. God never curses when there is no reason for this decisive act of judgment, but Genesis 12:1–3, Deuteronomy 27:15–26, Jeremiah 48:10 and 2 Peter 2 show that these actions and attitudes can attract God's curse: anti-Semitism, following false religions, slighting our parents, mistreating our neighbours, having a wrong attitude to the helpless, bestiality, incest, murder, greed, disobedience and half-hearted obedience.

Genesis 3:14–15, 16 and 17–19 are the first three recorded curses by God. The serpent was cursed because he had tempted Eve; Eve was cursed because she had disobeyed God; and Adam was cursed because he had eaten from the forbidden tree. The curse on the serpent opposes the human race to the devil and his 'seed' – his posterity – and hints at humanity's ultimate victory. Wonderfully, God's first curse contains the *protoevangelium*, the first glimpse of salvation.

The curses on Adam and Eve were appropriate to their specific functions: the woman suffered as a mother and wife, and the man as a worker. To these falls from their original perfection were added death, in verse 19, and the loss of intimacy with God, in verse 23.

These Eden curses were God's response to sin and they are hereditary: in Romans 5, Paul draws the comparison between our solidarity in Christ as saviour and our solidarity in Adam as sinner. All humanity is still affected by these curses today – childbirth is just as painful for believers as for unbelievers, and thistles grow as vigorously in Christians' gardens as in their pagan neighbours'. These curses will cease to be operative only when the transforming day of Revelation 22:3 dawns and 'there shall be no more curse'.

The Old Testament contains two long passages which detail God's response to disobedience. The curses of the law, recorded in Leviticus 26 and Deuteronomy 28, are personal rather than hereditary, and Galatians 3:13 shows that Christ redeemed us from them on the cross. Leviticus 26 and Deuteronomy 28 are sobering chapters which make it devastatingly plain that destructive diseases are a curse, and that painful, wasting sicknesses are terrible afflictions, never divine blessings. They are signs of God's anger, not his pleasure. In fact, nowhere in the Bible does God promise to send sickness as a blessing to his obedient children, and nowhere is sickness described as a good thing. The scriptural principle is simple: health is good; sickness is bad.

The redeeming death of Jesus Christ is God's provision for our immediate release from the earthly consequences of the curse of the law, and for our ultimate release from the eternal consequences of the Eden curses. The cross of Calvary is the only legal basis of escape from any curse, for only Christ's substitutionary death has dealt with the sin of the whole world which caused these curses.

Nehemiah 13:2 looks back to Balaam and also peers forward to Calvary: 'But our God turned the curse into a blessing.' How did he do this? Galatians 3:1–14 provides the answer: 'Christ has redeemed us from the curse of the law, having becoming a curse for us (for it is written, "Cursed is everyone who hangs on a tree"), that the blessing of Abraham might come upon the Gentiles in Christ Jesus, that we might receive the promise of the Spirit through faith.' It is not just that Jesus was cursed by God when he was on the cross, but rather that he became a curse.

Romans 8:3 and Colossians 2:14 underline this fact. The High Priest was determined to kill Jesus, and could have done so easily on several occasions, but that would not have sufficed. He wanted Christ to be crucified so that the curse of Deuteronomy 21:22–23 could be attached to him – this would be the final, convincing evidence to the Jews that Jesus was a blasphemous impostor.

So to Christ went the curse, and to us comes the blessing. The message of Galatians 3 is not only that the cross is our means of escape from the effects of the curse of the law – which include suffering, sickness and premature death – but also that by the work of Christ on the cross we can exchange our cursed state for the blessing of Abraham.

By the cross the way has been made open for us to receive the quintessence of blessing – the promised Holy Spirit; and this blessing is only available because Christ became a curse for us. On the cross Christ exhausted all the evil which is due to the descendants of Adam. He did this so that those who believe may receive the anointing with the Holy Spirit – and share in the blessing due to him because of his perfect obedience. This is where all healing flows from, it is part of the divine blessing.

Abraham was the pioneer of the pathway from curse to blessing. He believed God and took him at his word despite the obstacles of human reasoning and glaring facts; his faith was imputed to him as righteousness. Our own justification is by grace through faith, not by trying harder! We are not saved by the good works that we do, we are saved to do God's good works; we are not saved by our obedience, but we are saved to create the possibility of obedience. Blessing – which includes healing and wholeness – is for the obedient, and faith in Christ moves us from the place of the certainty of a curse, to the position of the possibility of blessing.

The cross is the legal basis of this exchange. It is one thing, however, to have a right, and quite another to enjoy it. We may have been left a fantastic fortune of blessing, but there is a very crooked lawyer on the other side. God gave Israel the promised land, but they had to fight every inch of the way to possess it. So, too, we are called to spiritual warfare both to enable us to enjoy God's blessing of healing and wholeness, and to help others to move from their curse to his blessing.

P hysical and mental illness are obvious effects of sin, and all creation has become subject to them through the fall.

Sickness and death do not come from within God's nature, for they only began to develop as a result of Lucifer's, and then humanity's, fall. As we have seen, it is God's nature to bring salvation, not death, and to offer healing, not sickness. Of course, he judges sin when there is no repentance, but Romans 8:20–21 shows that he always does this in hope.

After Lucifer was ejected from heaven, he developed a rebellious kingdom characterised by sin, sickness and death, and these are all key parts of his wicked oppression of humanity. As Satan, he has established a thoroughly illegal kingdom, which God is allowing to flourish for a strictly limited period of time. It is only because God is working out a gracious greater purpose – which we do not know or understand – that the just sentence he passed on Satan at Calvary has not yet been fully imposed.

The devil, Satan, is the god of this age, and he controls the different elements of our age through his weapons of sin, sickness, selfishness, disease, demonisation and death. Christian ministry is essentially about destroying every work of the devil, and we are called to smash the weapon of sickness through healing. We can do this because God's rule is greater and more powerful than Satan's, yet this wonderful truth forces us to address the fact that all sickness must, therefore, be allowed by God.

I do not believe that 'God allowing sickness' is the same as 'God willing sickness'. There is a vital difference between these two ideas which has deep implications about God's nature and for Christian ministry. If God really does will sickness, he cannot be a good God and we would be working against him by trying to bring healing. In fact, any believer who thinks that sickness expresses God's perfect will should really reject every form of healing and eagerly embrace every type of sickness!

I do not believe that God ever directly wills sickness, but his greater power means that he does allow it, and the Bible shows that he occasionally uses it for his greater purposes. Many leaders – including myself – often use the expression 'God's permissive will' when we mean 'God's allowing'. Perhaps we need to make it clear what we mean by this, as I suspect some believers have thought that we are speaking about God's perfect will.

God's perfect will for humanity is perfect health and wholeness. This is visible in creation and the cross and will be seen at the resurrection at the last day. Sickness, sin and death are not part of his perfect will; however, he allows them temporarily to flourish because he cherishes free will – and the love which flows only from this – so highly. We will never develop a truly Christian understanding of sickness until we appreciate the critical difference between God 'willing' something and God 'allowing' it.

We see the distinction in the story of Job, which has been recorded at enormous length in the Scriptures to help us develop a better understanding of sickness. In the book of Job, God is so confident of his greater power that, because of his hidden agenda, he allows Satan to afflict his servant with sickness. Even though God knows he is in ultimate control, it is patently clear that he does not directly will sickness on Job. It is vital we ensure that Job 2:3–7 is ingrained in our understanding of sickness.

Some people can appreciate the distinction between 'allowing' and 'willing' when it is clear that God has allowed the devil to impose sickness. But they find it hard to see the distinction in the Old Testament healing miracles where God himself imposes sickness as a curse, and in passages like Exodus 9:8–9, Psalm 6:1–4, 32:3–5, 51:7–8 and 1 Corinthians 11:29–32. They want to know what the difference is between God 'using' sickness and God 'willing' sickness. If he uses it or curses with it, they say, he must will it.

In these passages, though, God uses sickness as a means of encouraging Abimelech, Miriam, Hezekiah, the Egyptians, the psalmist, the Corinthians, and so on, to repent. He curses sin so that he can bless repentance. His perfect will is life, not death or sickness; and the sickness he uses is merely a temporary means to help people experience his perfect will and blessing.

When these sorts of instances occur today, the healing of the sickness is still wrapped in repentance. Sometimes the healing may be a natural response to turning away from a sinful, unhealthy lifestyle. At other times, it may be a supernatural consequence of confession and repentance – as in James 5:16. We should, however, be very slow to judge and make uncompromising statements about whether God is doing this in any particular case.

Some believers recognise the difference between 'using' and 'willing', but they have a considerable problem with the idea of God using sickness – which is why they blame the devil for everything. They wonder how the perfect, holy, health-giving God can possibly be associated with something which is essentially a consequence of sin. Yet this is the very point of the incarnation, the atonement, even the in-dwelling Spirit.

God in his grace is not only transcendent, he is also immanent. He is God with us – in a sinful world and in our sick bodies. Because of his great love, and to achieve the redemption of his creation, he has become deeply involved with the world of sin, so deeply involved that his Son became a curse for us. It is not God's will that we should ever sin, but in his grace he uses us even when we are sinful. And the Father's occasional use of sickness to bring about repentance and life is but a small thing compared to the Son's total identification with sin and sickness to earn our eternal life and perfect healing.

Just as healing is a sign pointing to the Creator and to more important matters of his kingdom, so sickness is a sign which points to the destroyer. However, we should never confuse any sickness with Satan himself, or any disease with a particular demon. Sickness is a weapon or work of the enemy; it is a manifestation of his activity. I am sure that demons are at work bringing disease and sickness, but no sickness is a demonic personification or a diabolical disguise.

Sickness is merely one aspect of Satan's kingdom, which also includes sin, darkness, hatred, falsehood and death. And all of these are opposed by God's kingdom of purity, truth, health, light, love and life. Most of the difficulties we face in our understanding of healing and sickness stem from the fact that we live in an overlap between these two kingdoms. Although, in Christ, we have been legally transferred from the kingdom of darkness to the kingdom of light, from the rule of Satan to the rule of God, we are still subject to many aspects of Satan's kingdom because it is being allowed to remain active until its final destruction.

The Jews had waited for centuries for the coming of the kingdom of God. Their anointed prophets had proclaimed and predicted it. They thought that it would be an age when God's power would be visible and dynamic, and that this age would begin when the Messiah – the Christos, the Anointed One – was revealed.

But the way in which the kingdom came was totally unexpected. The Jews thought that the kingdoms of this world would come to an end when the Messiah came, and that he would usher in the new kingdom of God. However, God's kingdom came as a mystery without any of the outward demonstrations and unambiguity of his glory. On the one hand, Jesus taught that he was the King of Israel, yet on the other hand he wore ordinary working clothes and spoke with an uneducated Galilean accent. Jesus did not look or sound like the expected Messiah, and was revealing a present form of the kingdom which had come in advance of its final form when God's unambiguous glory would fill the world.

When Jesus came he did not directly replace Satan's kingdom with God's; he released God's kingdom – the personal rule and reign of God – into Satan's. We can say that the rightful ruler invaded the rebellious kingdom and sought to re-establish God's personal rule. Only when Jesus returns will he consummate his kingdom and close Satan's. We are called to live and minister in the overlap between the two kingdoms – to be ruled personally by God while living in Satan's world. This means that we have the holy responsibility of introducing truth into a time of error, love into a land of hatred, service into an era of selfishness, and healing into a world of sickness.

The great secret of God's kingdom is that – in advance of the full and final form which will totally overcome Satan's kingdom at the last day – there is a present form which has decisively broken into the kingdom of sickness and death. As a result, we can have a thoroughly positive approach to healing as a dynamic of God's kingdom; but we must also acknowledge that we are living in Satan's world and so are likely to have some failures in our dealings with sickness.

Passages like Revelation 21:3–5 and 1 John 3:2–3 reveal that sin, sickness and death will all be totally eradicated in the future manifestation of God's kingdom; and Matthew 12:28 shows us there are many signs that the kingdom is here now. The kingdom of Satan has been invaded; it is being pushed back. And it is the present function of God's kingdom to deal with the different aspects of Satan's evil kingdom. This involves preaching, teaching, witnessing, holy living, humble service – and every possible form of healing.

When God's kingdom – his personal rule – came in with Jesus, the whole nation of Israel was stirred up as preaching and healing swept across vast areas. We can say that his preaching – and that of the early Church – introduced truth and light into the domain of lies and darkness, and that his healing brought health and life where before there had been only sickness and death.

The coming of Christ in a nation can be just as visible and effective today as it was in Israel and Asia Minor. His words must be heard *and* his works must be seen if an accurate picture of the kingdom is to be seen in our locality. We know that healing will not be an optional extra in the future total manifestation of the kingdom of God, so we should surely expect that the healing of sickness will be an integral part of this preliminary 'overlap' stage of the kingdom. If there are no miraculous healings today – and there are unlikely to be any if we do not willingly partner God – it means that the present stage of the kingdom will not accurately represent the future form of the kingdom. It will not be the true 'foretaste' that it is meant to be.

# 12

# SIGNS AND WONDERS

In February 1996, one of London's newspapers had a front page headline which announced, 'Blind man's miracle'. Apparently, during the evening rush hour at an Underground station, a man with a white stick had fallen on to the live rails in front of an arriving train. Amazingly, he climbed out from under the wheels of the first carriage, scrambled back on to the platform, and got on another train which was just moving off from a neighbouring platform. Nobody was able to trace the man after the event to find out whether he had been hurt in any way.

London Underground inspectors say that the line was carrying 350 volts of power when he fell. They insist that he must have fallen into a safe two-foot wide space on the tracks, avoided the metal bars designed to scoop people forward so they do not go under trains, kept his head down as the train went over so he was not decapitated, and stayed perfectly still as the slightest sideways movement would have electrocuted him.

It was an extraordinary story, and the natural response of most people – including journalists – was to say, 'It's a miracle.' Strangely, in the same week, exactly the same phrase was being used in an advertisement on British television. In the advert, two Spanish towns were cleaning outsize paella pans, using ten men with brooms to scrub off the grease. One town was using 'ordinary' washing-up liquid, and the other was using Fairy Liquid. Of course, the team using Fairy Liquid finished first and joined in the evening festivities, while the other team was still scrubbing the pans late into the night. An on-screen visual showed a bottle of Fairy Liquid with the words, 'It's a miracle!' An actor repeated this phrase in a voice-over with the qualification 'on grease'.

Nobody seems to have had the slightest problem with describing either of these matters as miracles. Everybody knows that, with regard to the blind man, the word 'miracle' was used to describe something 'extraordinary' – a set of circumstances which could even have been unprecedented – and in the context of the advert, 'miracle' was meant to mean something 'extremely powerful'.

In contrast, many people in western Europe have enormous problems when the word 'miracle' is used in a religious context. They are comfortable calling an extraordinary escape a 'miracle' and a powerful cleaning liquid 'miraculous' – even after officials have explained what happened at the track and scientists have offered their formula for cutting through grease. Yet most modern people are uncomfortable with the thought of miraculous healing, and any possible explanation for an extraordinary and powerful healing is taken as immediate 'proof' that it was not a miracle.

A few years ago, one of our leaders was diagnosed by his doctor as suffering from osteoarthritis. He was prescribed anti-inflammatory drugs, but did not feel that these were helping him. At one of our meetings, he was sitting in the congregation when he was picked out by a visiting speaker. Under the anointing of the Spirit, the visitor – who did not know the man or anything about his condition – quoted word for word what his doctor had said and stated that he was suffering from arthritis. The leader was prayed for, and was instantly fully healed. He has had no pain or discomfort since and has not taken any more of the anti-inflammatory drugs.

I call this a miracle. By this, I mean it was 'extraordinary' in that the visitor exactly repeated what the doctor had said, and 'powerful' in that the leader got better when he was prayed for. I do not know, or mind, whether the diagnosis of arthritis was correct or not, or whether the anti-inflammatory drugs played a part in the cure. I am simply delighted that his pain and discomfort stopped and did not return. Even if a surgeon could offer a convincing medical explanation, I would still consider what happened a miracle because the man's healing *coincided* with the prayer and not with the medical treatment. In these sorts of instances, Christians use the word 'miracle' in exactly the same way as the journalists who described the blind man's 'miraculous' escape.

Yet, time and again, when Christians suggest that a miracle has occurred a critic will maintain that there must have been a wrong diagnosis by a doctor, or that hospital tests were misinterpreted or improperly carried out, or that there has been a sudden remission, or that psychological factors were at work, or that medical treatment has taken effect more quickly than expected, or that there was a delayed response to the drugs. It is as if sceptics believe that a possible explanation actually negates the idea of a miracle. This is a common, but completely mistaken, idea.

Establishing the process behind a miracle does not remove the miraculous element, for the significance of a miracle usually lies in its timing and place rather than its occurrence. All sorts of 'natural' explanations have been offered for the parting of the Red Sea, but – even if these were accepted – the miracle is surely that the parting occurred when the Israelites were standing on the shore and Moses was praying, and that the waters returned while the Egyptians were crossing.

In the same way, there can usually be several explanations for the healing of a man or woman when prayed for by an anointed believer. Most sick people in western Europe – it is not always the same in Africa, Asia and Latin America – have probably been treated by a doctor, perhaps even assessed by a specialist. They might have been misdiagnosed. The drugs they are taking may suddenly have started to work after a period of not seeming to help. Psychological factors could be involved. The miracle, surely, is that the pain diminished and the symptoms started to vanish when they were prayed for. It is as absurd for critics to ignore the extraordinary timing and the divine power released through prayer as it is for believers to assert that the Creator does not use the medical and psychological processes he made.

The English word 'miracle' comes from the Latin root *miror* which means 'to wonder at'. In Latin, *mirus* meant wonderful, *miraculosus* was the word for something very surprising, and a *miraculum* was an object of wonder. Modern English diction-aries define a 'miracle' as 'a marvellous event' or 'a remarkable occurrence'. As we have seen, this is still the everyday understanding. The blind man's escape at the tube station was wonderful; it was a marvellous event; it was a remarkable occurrence – it was a miracle.

Christian people, therefore, are entirely consistent with good English when they use the word 'miracle' to describe a powerful divine healing or an unusual improvement. Of course, we should not use the word for every answer to prayer, but should reserve it for those extraordinary occasions when people have been genuinely inspired to awe or 'wonder' by an activity of God. Our leader's cure from osteoarthritis was wonderful; it was a marvellous event; it was a remarkable occurrence – surely this means that, in plain English, it was also a miracle. So why is there such intense opposition to our use of the word 'miracle' when somebody is healed? Why does western society have such a problem with the idea of the miraculous?

It seems to me that there are four main problems which, as Christians, we need to recognise and address. These problems are tightly woven together, and our thoughts about any one directly affect our ideas about the others.

First, there is the widespread influence of scepticism in western society which means that many people will not even consider the possibility of a divine element. For these people, everything is coloured by their religious belief that God does not exist and that miracles do not occur and have never occurred. This belief would be intellectually credible only if all reports of miracles were known to be false, but we can know that all reports are false only if we know that miracles have never occurred. This is circular reasoning which is entirely illogical.

Then there is the common idea that science is unlimited and can explain everything. Even if people are mystified by a particular physical improvement, most have faith that science will soon come up with the right answer. The old wrong idea of a 'God of the gaps' has been replaced by the modern fiction that 'science will fill all the gaps'. Popular scepticism, mixed with this unreasoned belief that science has no limits, is naively intolerant and will not even consider the possibility of divine healing.

Third, there is the difference – the gulf even – between the Christian and medical approach to healing which we glanced at in chapter six. Ministers and doctors do not always realise that they ask fundamentally different questions when faced with sickness and healing. As a result, there is tremendous confusion as critics commonly think that Christians are trying to provide scientific answers to scientific questions, when we are in fact providing theological answers to theological questions. Dialogue is virtually impossible under these circumstances, as scientists cannot answer our questions and we cannot answer theirs. But, thank God, there are some scientists who are committed Christians who are helping us to move towards a much more complete understanding of healing.

Finally, there is an almost complete lack of agreement about the basic definition of a miracle. Sceptics have succeeded in popularising some criteria for a healing miracle which most thinking Christians should utterly reject. By suggesting criteria, opponents of divine healing appear to be reasonable and open-minded, but they know that their criteria are almost impossible to fulfil.

Sceptics are trying to make sure that Christians reserve the word 'miracle' for occasional, unprecedented and unexplainable events. In their love of the scientific, they are trying to create a category of events which is rigidly defined – that is how they think. But, in their fear of the uncontrollable divine factor, they are trying to make the category so small that nothing will fit in it!

These days, sceptical critics usually demand six factors before they will acknowledge a miracle.

1. The condition must be correctly identified or diagnosed.

2. It must be incurable.

3. It must never remit – never have been known to get better of its own accord.

4. It must have had no previous treatment.

5. The cure must be instantaneous.

6. The cure must be complete.

These criteria have become widely accepted simply because authoritative-sounding sceptics have constantly repeated them and Christians have been too timid to expose them as the absurdity that they are. For example, most of Jesus' miracles fail to meet all the criteria – some of the people he healed had been previously treated; a few of his cures were not instantaneous or immediately complete; several of the diseases he healed were not incurable; hardly any of them had been identified to acceptable sceptical standards; and none of his cures were medically or scientifically verified! If even Jesus' miracles have to be disallowed, we can be certain that most of ours will also be rejected.

According to the criteria, most third world miracles must be rejected as the people often live too far away from a doctor for their condition to have been medically identified. In this country, for the criteria to be fulfilled, sick people must visit a doctor and their condition must be correctly diagnosed, but the doctor must then neglect to treat them in any way. By the criteria, it cannot be a miracle if the person has not visited a doctor; and, in reality, it cannot be a miracle if a doctor has been visited for the doctor will have given treatment.

Equally, the criteria assume that God is never involved in remission, that God does not work alongside medical processes, that a 99 per cent recovery is not a miracle, that a cure over a couple of hours is not miraculous, and that a miraculous cure of an incurable disease means no miraculous cure of that particular disease can ever again be deemed a miracle.

We do not have to push this approach too far to see just how absurd it is. Logically, the only cure which the criteria would allow to be classified as a miracle is when a limb which had been completely severed in an accident instantly and fully regrew after prayer – as long as the prayer was offered after the ambulance had arrived and before the patient reached the hospital. If, however, a limb had been surgically amputated, any new growth would not be miraculous as the limb would have been medically treated!

While ministering in Brazil, I have often met with a Christian surgeon who works at Osvaldo Cruz, one of São Paulo's leading hospitals, as a gynaecologist. In 1997, he introduced me to one of his patients who had experienced an amazing healing two years earlier – but I guarantee that the accepted criteria would not recognise even her cure as miraculous. Several years earlier, she had had a caesarean section during which her intestine had been perforated. This led to an intestinal infection, and she was operated on eight times at various hospitals in Brazil. She was in a terrible state by the time she was sent to the doctor's clinic at Osvaldo Cruz Hospital. By then – on 21 March 1995 – she had a tumour growing in the place where her left ovary and fallopian tube had been removed. The doctor scanned her and, using his advanced computer equipment, measured the tumour at 49.5 cubic centimetres. He believed that her abdomen was in too bad a condition for any more surgery and decided to try radiotherapy instead. But first he asked the patient – who was herself a believer – if they could pray and ask Jesus to help.

In the short period of time between seeing the doctor and returning for her first course of treatment, the patient attended a praise service. One of the lady leaders at the meeting sensed that the Spirit was saying that there was a woman present who had a tumour on her left side which he wanted to heal. She announced this, and went on to describe exactly what the doctor had said. The sick woman went forward and the leaders prayed for her. When she returned to the hospital on 26 April 1995, a second scan showed no trace of the tumour in her abdomen. It had completely disappeared.

As Christians ministering in a sceptical world, it is important that – as in this case – we obtain medical verification of healings whenever possible. This woman's 'before' and 'after' scans honour God and add credibility to the ministry of God's partners. However, we must recognise that, even when there is an unambiguous improvement or cure, the prevailing climate of opinion will not interpret the cure as a miracle. If there has been any medical intervention or treatment, sceptics will automatically reject the possibility of a miracle.

I believe that Christians should reject these meaningless criteria and insist on using the word 'miracle' in the linguistically correct sense of meaning 'an extraordinary act of power which has inspired wonder' – while making it clear that the power is God's and God's alone. This means, though, we do need to check that an extraordinary act has occurred and that divine power is involved before we start claiming a miracle. There are a few gullible people in most churches, and some may be taken in by false, or over-stated, claims. This does not honour God and does nothing to advance the cause of the kingdom.

There was a British case in early 1997, when a man who had been seated in a wheelchair for several months started to walk during a service at a Pentecostal church, and claimed that he had been miraculously healed. Many local people were excited, but the minister wisely checked what had happened. Before making any claims, he wanted to find out whether there had been a genuine act of power. He quickly discovered that the man was a fraud: he had been using the wheelchair to attract charitable gifts, and was now claiming a miracle to attract even more attention to himself.

Christians also believe that every miracle is a 'sign' as well as a 'wonder', that it is a pointer or witness to God and to aspects of his kingdom. This is something which sceptics and scientists simply cannot understand. We use the word 'miracle' in these two ways because the word which is usually translated 'miracle' in the New Testament literally means 'power', and because it is very widely associated in the Scriptures with 'signs and wonders'. The healing miracles of Jesus were 'wondered' at by those who witnessed them, and they saw them as communicating God's power. But the Gospels show that the miracles also had a far deeper meaning – they were 'signs' of the presence of the kingdom of God.

We are mistaken if we try to understand or define miracles in a narrow, scientific way, as this means we must concentrate only on examining the physical features of every event. Of course, as we have seen, we must examine the external facts to check that something extraordinary really has occurred, but we do this so we can be confident that God is at work in some way. On their own, healing miracles are always *wonder*-full acts of power – regardless of whether God has intervened solely in a supernatural way or worked through natural medical and psychological processes as well. But, in the context of Christ's continuing ministry on earth, they are also *signs* pointing to a greater reality. And, as we have seen throughout this book, this sign element is crucially important.

When a miraculous healing takes place, the person who receives it is normally aware of a cluster of events which occur beyond the physical change. In fact, the physical healing is often the least important part of the miracle. I frequently find that people who are healed describe a new sense of God's presence or a new awareness of God's forgiveness or a deeper knowledge of assurance or a massive increase in hope or a new way of living as a family. They are very grateful for the wonder, but they are preoccupied with the reality towards which the sign was pointing.

Ten years ago, one of our present members lost most of his sight while serving in the US Marines as a sniper. He was discharged, sent to a rehabilitation centre for the blind, and was told by three leading specialists that he would be completely blind by the time he was twenty-four. His grandparents, who were committed Christians, started to pray for his healing – and for a wider work of God in his life. Early this year, when he was just thirty, his eye surgeon was using words like 'miraculous', 'regenerated', 'new condition' to describe the improvement in his sight. But he himself was far more interested in using 'regenerated' and 'new life' in a quite different way! His healing had pointed him to the healer and a far more important healing.

Before becoming a Christian, a lady had suffered from epilepsy for fifteen years. Christians prayed for her condition, and she believed that she was healed. In fact, she was so convinced about her healing that without telling her doctor she stopped taking the medicine which controlled her epilepsy. This was particularly dangerous and ill-advised. Fortunately, a short while later, she visited Kensington Temple for healing prayer and one of our leaders sent her straight to her neurologist to check whether or not she had been healed.

At first the neurologist told her that there was no chance of a cure, but – after extensive tests – she was told that the chances of her ever having another fit were now lower than those of the average person. Ten years later, she remains completely free from epilepsy, is a deeply committed Christian, and rejoices in all the changes which have come through her healing. She has been able to drive a car, and – after a letter from her doctor explained what had happened – her motor insurance more than halved in price!

We can be sure that, whenever God comes to heal, there will be unexpected changes in the person's life – and in the lives of those around. Every divine healing wonderfully boosts the hope of many people who see it or hear about it, for every miracle is a sign pointing to God's compassionate power and to the perfect final healing before us. We miss the significance of these 'signs' if we are preoccupied with defending a miracle in strictly scientific terms or with trying to make it fit with some sceptic's mistaken criteria.

One of the problems with Christians accepting the secular understanding of 'a miracle' is that it reserves the word for occasional, unprecedented and unexplainable events. This narrow idea places God's healing activity entirely in the extraordinary, whereas my experience is that God's wonderful, powerful healings usually occur in situations which are untidy and complicated, and which involve both medicine and ministry. It seems clear to me that God heals gradually and instantly, mysteriously and obviously, and that his healing touch is felt within the painful as well as the painfree. If divine healing is to provide genuine hope for the millions of hurting people around us, we need constantly to affirm that the healing God is encountered as much in ordinary ways as in extraordinary ways.

I know that we will strengthen the hope of some people if our speaking about healing miracles is restricted to proving scientifically that God has intervened in a few spectacular stories. But I am sure that we will contribute so much more to healing, wholeness and hopefulness if we concentrate on pointing out that God is deeply involved in the usual and the everyday. This may mean that we should stop using the word 'miracle', as it is so misunderstood by people in western society. Instead, we could speak about 'complete healings' and 'considerable improvements', or 'wonderful healings' and 'significant improvements'.

At the moment, our witness is hampered by the popular highly restricted understanding of the word 'miracle' when it is used in a religious context. If we say that a miracle has happened, ordinary people expect to see something which is instantaneous, total and medically unexplainable. When they see something which is merely wonderful and unusual, and where there has been some medical treatment, they question our credibility and integrity – and our witness to the truth is compromised. For the sake of the gospel, we should make our understanding of miracles very much clearer so that ordinary people really do know what we mean when we are using the word 'miracle'.

*E*ven if we do explain ourselves rather more clearly, we will still face a considerable problem as the way our society thinks about signs and wonders has been shaped by ideas and assumptions which have emerged over hundreds of years.

Until five centuries ago, healing miracles were considered to be an inevitable part of living in a world which had been created by God and was still actively controlled by him. But today miracles are widely seen as an intellectual embarrassment. People are now so impressed by the regularity of the world that any story which is unusual is perceived to be an invention.

The change in attitudes began over four hundred years ago, when European thinkers started to realise that the same event could be interpreted in more than one way. Until then, *how* and *why* questions had always been answered in the same way: rain came so that crops could flourish; seeds fell so that new plants could grow; disasters and diseases arrived as signs of divine displeasure; rainbows were sent to remind us of God's promise; the Red Sea parted because God loved the Jews – and so on.

Science developed through ignoring *why* questions and concentrating instead on asking and answering *how* questions.

Newton discovered gravity through the radical idea of asking himself, 'How did that happen?' rather than, 'Why did it fall on me? What does this mean?' It is hard for us to appreciate just how innovatory this change in approach was. The growing scientific preoccupation with *how* slowly led to an emphasis on the uniformity and predictability of natural events, and – by the late seventeenth century – God's actions were beginning to be restricted to the ever-decreasing gaps in knowledge.

In western Europe, we still suffer from this divide between *how* and *why*. When people today consider something like the parting of the Red Sea – or the healing of our leader from arthritis – they automatically ask themselves, 'How did it happen?' It does not occur to them to ask, 'Why did it happen?' or 'What does it mean?' People now think either that the answer to *how* is also the answer to *why* or that it negates the *why*. And in this their scepticism is intellectually flawed.

I suspect that we will never be able to speak effectively to our society about healing miracles until we make it clear that we are asking and answering different questions – and that both *how* and *why* questions are equally valid, equally valuable, and that neither should be avoided or confused.

As Christian ministers, we need to ensure that we are addressing the *why* questions – for most of us are not qualified to answer the *how* questions of healing. Critics rightly mock us when we give a naive or simplistic answer to a scientific *how* question. We, in turn, need to be much more assertive in insisting that they should be intellectually open to complementary causes and complementary explanations for a miracle, that they should face up to theological and moral questions, and should recognise their lack of qualification to answer them.

During the seventeenth century, scientists started to lay down the 'laws of nature' and teach that the world was closed and self-regulating. They said that God was merely the 'First Cause', and that he could intervene only by breaking or suspending 'natural laws'. Some scientists went further than this and argued that natural laws could not be broken, and that – therefore – miracles could not happen. This is still a very popular idea today, but it is based entirely on an inaccurate or incomplete picture about God.

People who hold this view believe that God – if he exists – is essentially transcendent and that he occasionally breaks into the world to intervene. As Christians, we know that this is far from the full biblical picture, for he is also the immanent God who is deeply involved in sustaining the world he made by the processes he designed.

I am sure that God does intervene supernaturally. But I am convinced that he also works actively through natural, genetic, selective and random processes. This means that miracles are a necessary but humanly unpredictable consequence of a God who is a wilful, transcendental interferer, *and* that they are also a necessary but humanly unpredictable consequence of a God who holds everything in being. If you think about this hard enough, you will see that it is true!

Because people did not – and still do not – understand God's immanent nature, the nineteenth-century theories of Darwin convinced most people that the ideas of purpose and created pattern were wrong, and that – therefore – it was a waste of time asking *why* questions. As far as they are concerned, evolution proves that there is no Creator; and, as there is no Creator, *why* questions have no meaning. Most scientists do not stop and consider even the possibility that a Creator could create through a creative evolutionary process! The massive scientific advances of the twentieth century have built on this, and have led most people to conclude that science has no boundaries, and that scientists will soon have an explanation for everything and will eventually be able to do anything.

A number of false assumptions have arisen from these ideas, and it is these which underscore the popular rejection of miracles. For example, most people – educated and uneducated alike – now unthinkingly believe that events have only a single cause, and that every event can be fully explained if that cause is known. This is logically and intellectually wrong.

An oil painting can be explained in terms of the distribution of paint pigments or in terms of the artist's intention, and a piece of music can be explained by sound waves or the composer's design. Both explanations refer to the same thing, but they complement rather than conflict. In the same way, a healing miracle may be explained in terms of medical or psychological processes *as well as* the actions of a divine sustainer of the physical world.

This false insistence on a single explanation leads both believers and unbelievers astray. If a possible medical explanation can be found for a miracle, unbelievers wrongly conclude that it is the sole cause and that all other factors are therefore irrelevant. If prayer has been made, believers stupidly think that God cannot have worked though any natural or medical process. Many of the barren arguments between Christians and critics have been based on their joint error of believing in a single explanation or a sole cause.

When God works immanently through a natural process, there will be more than one way of explaining the event; however, the religious view will be more complete. When God intervenes supernaturally in the life of a person who has been medically treated, there will not only be a couple of valid explanations, there will also be more than one cause. But when God works supernaturally, and there is no medical cause, there will be only one valid explanation and a single cause.

In such a case, when there is no known cause or medical explanation for a healing which occurred simultaneously with prayer, most ordinary people believe that – given enough time – scientists will eventually identify the cause and come up with the correct explanation. The false assumption here is the modern idea that science has no limits.

Yet there are hosts of questions which science cannot answer and which no conceivable advances of science will ever empower it to answer. 'Why did everything begin?' 'Why are we all here?' 'Why am I alive?' 'What happens to me when I die?' These sorts of questions make sense to the people who ask them, and our answers make sense to those of us who offer them. Science has largely rejected these sorts of *why* questions because it cannot answer them – and because they remind us that there is a genuine limit to scientific understanding.

The 'wonder' element of miracles always triggers *why* questions in humans – which is why the Bible considers them to be signs. We can understand them and make sense of them only by asking questions like, 'Why has this happened?' 'What does this mean?' 'What should we do?' If we neglect to ask or answer *why* we are implicitly rejecting the sign element inherent in miracles. Modern believers who focus on the world's *how* questions of healing are often those who stray down the blind alley of technique.

The 'sign' or *why* element of miracles means that they are impossible to prove or disprove by normal scientific criteria. All truly honest scientists admit that they can *never* answer the question, 'Is this a miracle?' The most that a doctor may be able to tell us is whether there has been an improvement or not, but either we accept the possibility of miracles by faith, or we deny them by faith.

Yet even when a doctor has determined that there has been no change in the person's physical condition, there may still have been a miraculous healing. All doctors know that they can find nothing physically wrong with many of the people who come to them claiming to be ill, and – equally – that they can find no physical improvement in others who claim to have been medically healed.

Although sceptical critics may loudly claim that many cures – both medical and miraculous – have a psychological explanation, they usually keep quiet about the fact that recent developments in the understanding of psychosomatic disorders have dealt a death blow to their idea of a single cause for events and a single explanation for healing.

The reality of scepticism means that we must not naively assume that people are going to fall down and worship God whenever they witness a healing, or that they will start considering the divine option because scientific advances have shown that the body interacts with non-physical elements of life.

Scepticism based in rationalism has such a hold on people that it blinds them to what is plainly before them. There will always be those who say, 'Nothing has been proved. Give us more time, we will be able to explain it without God.' But even those who have moved away from rationalism to a more open, post-modern way of viewing the world will also remain sceptical. They may be convinced that something extraordinary and powerful has happened, but instead of accepting the Christian claim of a wonderful, powerful healing in Jesus' name they will look for other explanations.

We can be sure that each genuine miracle will always be a fantastic wonder, but we must not forget that it will also be only a sign – and as such it is very easily ignored. In our excitement at experiencing or observing God's power, we must remember that there is no guarantee that a healing miracle will ever convert anyone.

# 13

# SCEPTICISM AND PSYCHOSOMATIC DISORDERS

In recent years, several television programmes have been broadcast in Britain which have been so influenced by popular scepticism that they have been less than honest in their arguments and conclusions. These programmes were meant to be rigorous investigations of Christian healing miracles, and they all concluded that no case had been presented which was capable of convincing independent medical opinion that a miracle had taken place.

Alarmingly, the programme makers did not seem to be aware of their own assumptions about a single explanation and a science without limits. They made it clear that a miracle could be accepted only if it could be shown that no natural explanation could ever be found, and then suggested that anything currently unexplained was awaiting further scientific investigation. Clearly there could be no admission of a miracle while holding this view! Yet the makers could not grasp that their conclusion was inevitable before the first case was considered.

One of the programmes focused on a woman who had been healed during a Christian evangelistic meeting and was now free from crippling back pain. Her doctor was not a religious man and admitted that he was unsure how a miracle could be defined – so he was careful not to call his patient's healing a miracle. He knew that he could not identify something when he did not know what he was looking for.

His medical examination showed that there had been no

change in the woman's underlying physical condition, but that she was totally free from pain. He admitted that this was 'a very surprising and interesting improvement or alteration'. The doctor was medically qualified to comment on the improvement, but theologically unqualified to assess whether it was a miracle. Of course, the programme makers focused on his reluctance to call the improvement a miracle – their position was that it cannot be a miracle unless an 'independent medical opinion' is convinced that it is a miracle! They just did not grasp that no medical expert can ever be truly independent – in the sense of being intellectually distant and disinterested – of the miracle debate. Someone who is sceptical is bound to conclude that any improvement is not miraculous.

The programme – unaware of its intellectual blinkers – inevitably focused entirely on *how* questions. It glossed over the woman's medically agreed improvement and concentrated on asking how she could possibly have become free from pain. The programme makers plumped for a psychological explanation and decided that she was not really healed – her mind had simply blocked out her back pain. They ignored the facts that her cure had occurred during a Christian healing meeting, that she had not been expecting or looking for healing, that she had no allegiance to the Christian faith at the time of her healing, that she had continued without pain ever since, and that psychology is an incredibly inexact and contentious science. They dismissed her own explanation of God's power as empty faith – arguing that it was contradicted by the so-called certainties of science. And the possibility did not occur to anyone that God might have used natural psychological processes to enable her mind to block out her pain!

The woman's healing was explained away by means of an analogy which sceptics often use to dismiss divine healing. We were offered the picture of two crews in a boat race. At the end of the race, the defeated crew are slumped over their oars, exhausted and demoralised. 'Now imagine,' the sceptic says, 'what would happen to the beaten crew if they heard that their opponents had been disqualified. It would look just as if they had been supernaturally healed of exhaustion and demoralisation. That's what happens,' they say, 'at a Christian healing meeting. People are told that they have been healed, and they so want to believe it that they start feeling better. It's psychological suggestion; it's mind over matter.'

There are two problems with this analogy. First, the crew would know that they were merely feeling elated and were only temporarily distracted from their pain by their joy; and, second, they would feel their aching muscles on the following day. In contrast, the woman being investigated felt elated only after she realised that her pain had completely stopped. Her sense of joy and well-being was a consequence of being cured, not the cause of it; and she was not only free from pain on the following day, she has been fully pain-free ever since.

The programmes were supposed to be open investigations, yet the makers would not admit to there being two possible explanations – which could be complementary rather than opposed. The astonishing ease with which the programmes dismissed the possibility of God's power exposed the intellectual barrenness of modern scepticism. Sadly, the considerable impact of the programmes in Britain – and the way their conclusions were unthinkingly accepted by most people, including many Christians – revealed the cancerous grip that scepticism holds on western society.

Tragically, scepticism has affected most sections of the Church for much of the last two centuries. It is not only unbelieving scientists who do not accept supernatural divine healing, many church leaders are equally disbelieving. They usually hide their scepticism in a thicket of theology and argue that, although miracles did happen in New Testament times, they ceased once the Church had been established. This is an argument which is usually put forward by leaders more to justify the gulf between their personal experience and the Scriptures than because it can be justified from the Scriptures!

The problem with this is that, once such an absolute position is taken, every reported miracle must either be explained as an invention or accredited to a power other than God. This was not too difficult when few miracles were being reported among churches in western Europe, but the sheer weight of evidence in the last ten years has meant that the 'cessationist' approach is losing credibility among many church leaders.

*W* hen Christians speak about a particular healing, the first thing sceptics usually want to know is what was wrong with the person. They will accept medical verification of a cure only if there has been medical identification of the condition. 'If we don't know what was wrong,' they say, 'how can we tell whether or not the person has been healed?' This approach means that they tend to be particularly suspicious about the signs and wonders which God performs overseas.

I suspect that such scepticism is more instinctive than reasoned, and that sceptics reject our testimony simply because their rigid world view assumes that anything unusual must be invented. However, they usually base their scepticism on the belief that most miraculous cures in Africa, Asia and Latin America occur among people who have never been treated by a doctor. They argue that we cannot trust a person's claims about healing when we cannot know whether they were really ill or not. Their implicit suggestion is that these people who claim to be healed were not genuinely ill in the first place.

It is generally true that many miraculous healings are among people who do not have access to medical care of western standards – though this is becoming less common. However, it is also generally true that most British sceptics have never seen a miraculous healing in Asia, Africa or Latin America, and have no comprehension of how convincing many healings are. Most people in western Europe have a completely false picture of the ministry of divine healing in less-developed countries; in fact, the reality is far closer to a New Testament scene than most of what we see.

In October 1992, a journalist friend was working in India when he wrote the following account of the first Pentecostal healing crusade to be held in Calcutta:

Between five thirty and six thirty the crowd poured in. There'd been no advertising except for a few banners and posters. Nobody had heard of the evangelist before that week – if my name had been on the publicity there would have been just as many people. Yet when the meeting began there were well over sixty thousand people in attendance.

Large numbers are notoriously difficult to estimate accurately. At British open-air marches there's always a massive discrepancy between the police and the organisers' figures. However, I've guessed the size of many a soccer crowd correctly and this one looked like a Cup Final size gathering.

But it wasn't the great mass of people in the distance which attracted my attention, it was the small groups huddling at the front. Every cripple and paralytic, every twisted limb and leprous body, every dying man, woman and child in Calcutta seemed to have gathered at the foot of the improvised stage.

It was a scene of near biblical proportions as the sick, the blind and the lame shuffled into the park hoping to be healed. People close to death were carried on antiquated stretchers. Children with grotesque deformities were pushed to the front. Men with sightless staring eyes and women with blood-stained saris tried to steal the best positions. Hundreds of them were just inches away from me, lying at my feet.

This was no charismatic party. This was not cheap entertainment for the saints. This was no fund-raising spectacle. This was religion at the raw edge of human experience; rugged faith rubbing shoulders with hopeless despair; real Christianity on trial for its claims.

I tell you, there are no doubts when people like these get healed. When I am confronted by an African family praising God at full volume because the father can see clearly for the first time in years, does anyone seriously suggest that I should reject their testimony just because his eye condition has not been diagnosed by a qualified doctor? If a Brazilian from a shanty town can hear clearly after prayer, or a hideous growth has vanished, or a chronic abdominal pain has ceased, or someone can walk properly for the first time, why should we reject their testimony just because they are poor and uneducated? They might not be able to say what they have been healed from – other than in the most general sense – but they can give reliable testimony to the improvement they have experienced. Of course, I accept that a tiny minority might invent ailments to help them beg more effectively or attract western aid, but few would have anything to gain from inventing a false cure.

In 1993, I was speaking at a series of meetings in the Hall of Arts in Cotonou – a small city in the tiny West African country of Benin. The meetings had been arranged by the Evangelical Council of Ministers in Cotonou and were attracting about 2,000 people, mostly from the poorest groups in one of Africa's poorest nations.

At the third meeting, I preached from Ezekiel 47 about the river of God which heals wherever it flows. God moved in remarkable power during that service, and several astonishing miracles occurred. A blind woman who was well known in the area was instantly healed, and a mini-revival quickly followed in the city as news of her cure spread on the African grapevine and local people came to check what had happened.

I do not know whether the woman had ever been treated or diagnosed by a doctor. But virtually everyone in her part of Cotonou knew her, knew that she was completely blind, and could see that she was cured. Nobody knew what had caused her blindness, but everyone knew that she received her sight during a Christian meeting at the Hall of Arts. There was widespread, long-standing, social proof that her condition was genuine, and obvious empirical evidence that her cure was instant and complete. It seems to me to be intellectually fraudulent to reject her testimony merely because she lives in a part of the world which lacks the medical resources to investigate the cause of her condition.

At the same meeting, another woman was cured of a massive growth in her stomach. She had been receiving treatment at the local hospital, and several nurses who had been caring for her at the hospital were also present at the service. These nurses saw her growth disappear during the meeting – and were just as astonished as their British counterparts would have been. They verified that she had been suffering from a serious stomach abnormality. They verified that her condition had vanished. And they praised God because his power seemed to be the only explanation of what had happened.

It was an extraordinary service; as I stood on the platform

it seemed to me that I could feel the river of God flowing around me. The Spirit kept on prompting me to call out more and more conditions of people who were being healed, more and more descriptions of people who were to be healed, more and more ailments which God was promising to heal. A local minister translated, and a group of colleagues from Kensington Temple prayed for people as they identified themselves. They then introduced the testimonies of the people who were obviously healed. It seemed to go on endlessly, and I felt that I needed to stop before I dropped. I knew that I had to get out of the way and leave the others to minister without me.

As I stepped off the platform, a huge wave of emotional relief washed over me – it felt as though the burden of the anointing had lifted because I was leaving the platform. After a few minutes of relaxing and drawing breath, I noticed that a teenage boy was standing next to me. Since birth he had been deaf and dumb, and his parents were waiting for me to pray for him to be healed. There were no lights or microphones, no watching crowds, no praying colleagues. It was just me and the boy. Everyone else was concentrating on what was happening on the platform. I offered a simple one-sentence prayer, 'Lord, heal this boy.' And *immediately* he began to hear and speak. It was so easy! And yet it is so hard for sceptical westerners to believe that God sometimes works like this. But he does, he really really does.

*O*ne of the problems with the sceptical insistence on knowing exactly what was wrong with people who claim that God has healed them, is that it tends to ignore the part played by psychosomatic illness. Anecdotal evidence from GPs suggests that over 50 per cent of the people who go to them are suffering from a significant psychosomatic disorder. As they admit that these are notoriously difficult to treat successfully, I think we must acknowledge that there is unlikely to be much hard physical evidence for the majority of healings we see in the Christian healing ministry. But this does not mean that the vast majority of divine healings are bogus! It simply means that illness and healing are far more complex that most people make out.

Psychosomatic medicine emphasises the unity of the mind

and the body – and the interaction between them – and stresses that psychological factors are important in the development of many diseases. Scientists are still debating whether these factors have a role in the initiation, the progression or the aggravation of a disease, or in a predisposition or reaction to a disease, or in delaying the recovery – or in all of these. Most believe that the influence of psychological factors varies from disorder to disorder.

The idea of a psychosomatic illness was first suggested 180 years ago, and some representatives from psychiatry and medicine have argued for over a century that the mind and the body overlap in many disorders. But it is only in the last twenty years that western scientists have begun to realise the extent to which psychological factors influence physical conditions.

Some people still think that people with psychosomatic disorders are not really sick and do not need medical attention. They think that people who want to be healed just need to 'pull themselves together'! The long controversy over ME, or 'yuppie flu', as it is sometimes disparagingly called, reflects this. But the symptoms of a psychosomatic illness often reflect changes in the body which are usually associated with physical damage and pain. For example, a peptic ulcer caused by stress is indistinguishable from an ulcer caused by a factor unrelated to stress such as the long-term heavy use of aspirin.

Even those doctors who are still suspicious about psycho-somatic illness agree that stress plays some part in causing, developing and delaying the recovery of many physical diseases. What seems to happen is that a stressful event or situation generates challenges to which an organism cannot adequately respond. It is now widely agreed that chronic stress can lead to ulcers, high blood pressure and heart disease; it can also impair the immune system and decrease the body's ability to fight bacteria and viruses.

M ost doctors estimate that emotional stress plays an important role in more than half of all medical problems. A scale has been developed which lists forty-three life events associated with varying amounts of disruption and stress in the average person's life. The death of a partner is given 100 units, divorce 73 units, imprisonment 63 units, marriage 50 units – and so on down to a holiday 15 units, Christmas 12 units and a parking ticket 11 units. Investigators have found that an accumulation of 200 or more life-changing units in any twelve-month period significantly increases the incidence of psychosomatic disorders.

The list of disorders which scientists consider to be liable to be affected by psychological factors is continually lengthening. These are just a small selection from the list of disorders which are currently classified as psychosomatic – acne, allergic reactions, angina pectoris, chronic pain syndromes, coronary heart disease, diabetes mellitus, duodenal ulcer, hay fever, herpes, high blood pressure, irritable colon, migraine, painful menstruation, rheumatoid arthritis, psoriasis, tuberculosis, vomiting and warts.

Five years ago, one of my friends was sent to a major London hospital because he had suddenly become deaf in his left ear. They found that this was due to a small brain tumour and he had to have urgent medical treatment. At that time he was involved in an unpleasant legal dispute over the custody of his children, and the consultant believed that the stress of the dispute had been a key factor in either the tumour's origin or in its development. My friend was told that it was vital for him to do everything possible to avoid stress as this was likely to exacerbate the condition and obstruct the healing.

He was treated for several months with radiotherapy, but the tumour did not appear to respond. The day before he was due to go into hospital for surgery, a small group of believers prayed with him for God's healing – praying especially that he would deeply experience God's peace. The following day a scan showed the first small improvement in his condition; surgery was postponed, and over the next six months the tumour slowly withered.

Most sceptics would still say that his improvement was *solely* due to the radiotherapy, but the insights of psychosomatic medicine – or behavioural medicine, as it is increasingly being called today – make it harder for them to deny the possibility of other influences. The significance of the timing of the prayer, and my friend's genuine experience of deep divine peace, and the medical recognition of the part played by the presence and absence of stress, and the probable intervention of God, should not be ignored.

Increasingly, doctors accept that extreme emotional and mental stress have considerable physical consequences, and that – therefore – complementary treatments like psycho-therapy and relaxation techniques are important parts of the healing process. Not only does this mean the beginning of the end for mistaken ideas about a sole cause for each illness and a single explanation for every cure, but it also helps us to appreciate that God's peace, God's love and God's presence are not just vaguely therapeutic but have a tangible physical impact.

**M** any of the testimonies from our members describe the way that they experienced God's healing at the time of their conversion. We will not be surprised by this if we believe that healing is a benefit of the cross, and that the mind, the body and the spirit form an inter-related unity in each person.

As scientists now concede that the body can be affected by the mind, it should not be too hard for them to accept the possibility that the mind and the body can also be affected by the spirit – or even by God's Spirit. But scepticism still largely rules supreme. The new interdisciplinary field of behavioural medicine may have been influenced by the move from rational-ism towards post-modernism, and be seeking to learn how social, psychological and biological variables combine to cause illness, and how they can be changed to promote health. Despite all this, only a tiny proportion of the British studies are considering a divine factor in healing. There does, however, seem to be slightly more openness in the United States.

One investigatory group has recently begun to consider the possibility that healing may be affected by prayer, but their research project has been constructed on scientific terms, like any other clinical tests. Their patients have been divided into groups. The first group are being told that they are being prayed for – and they are. The second group are being told that they are being prayed for – but they are not. The third group are being told that they are not being prayed for – and they are not. And the fourth group are being told that they are not being prayed for – but they are. The investigators are now monitoring the progress of the four groups and are wondering which one will make the best progress.

While their interest reveals an overdue openness, I suspect that their conclusions will be flawed. I doubt whether we can study God's power in this way, or restrict his sovereign workings by artificial constraints, or stop friends and family from praying if their loved ones are in the wrong group, or direct intercessory prayer by scientific whim rather than the Spirit's wisdom.

However, an early 1988 study by a cardiologist at San Francisco General Hospital had some interesting results. He took 393 patients in the coronary-care unit and randomly assigned half to be prayed for by 'born-again Christians' – the patients were not told of the experiment. Interestingly, the cardiologist found that those who were not prayed for were five times more likely to need antibiotics, and three times more likely to develop complications, than those who were prayed for.

A 1995 study at Dartmouth-Hitchcock Medical Center found that one of the best predictors of survival among 232 heart-surgery patients was the degree to which the patients said that they drew comfort and strength from religious faith. The death rate of those who had no religious faith was three times higher than that of those who did.

A recent survey of thirty years' research on blood pressure showed that churchgoers have an average 5 mm lower blood pressure than non-churchgoers – even after adjustments to account for smoking and other risk factors.

I find it entirely plausible that the transformation of our mind and spirit in conversion may have bodily consequences. One woman in our church had suffered from very severe period pains ever since she was a teenager. They continued long after she had recovered from giving birth, but vanished within months of becoming a Christian. Doctors now tell us that painful menstruation is a psychosomatic disorder, so it is surely likely that the divine peace she experienced in her life through conversion was the main cause of her bodily healing.

Sceptics dismiss incidents like this as psychological rather than divine, and we need to make it very clear that they are to be understood as God working immanently through the natural psychological processes he made rather than God intervening supernaturally from afar. He designed our bodies to respond to the presence of peace and a reduction in stress – so any physical disorders which are eased by relaxation therapy and psychotherapy are almost bound to respond to his perfect peace. These may not be miracles in a sceptic's restricted understanding of the term, but they are wonderful, powerful, life-changing healings which are precious to those who experience them.

Many people at our church describe God healing them from disorders like migraines, headaches, hay fever, back ache, bronchial asthma and general persistent pain. Psychosomatic or behavioural medicine now insists that all these conditions are considerably affected by psychological factors, and that medical treatment should be complemented by relevant, supportive psychotherapy and relaxation techniques.

This development has to support the Christian beliefs that spiritual healing affects the human body, and that God usually works through the ordinary processes he designed. When the Father fills our lives with his peace, his love, his faith, his hope and his joy, he not only affects our minds and our spirits, he also heals our bodies. This truth is so wonderful that we should celebrate it and proclaim it far more than we do.

M any Christian leaders have become so defensive about divine healing, so embarrassed by all the sceptics' attacks, that they have been effectively silenced. Yet Christian healing is not some quirkish claim peculiar to modern charismatics and loud American televangelists. It is the teaching of the whole Bible. It is basic to New Testament Christianity. It is a feature of every tradition of the Church, in every century and on every continent. And it is more common today than at any time – including the first century.

However, we must not forget that Christian healing is a sign of the kingdom – of God's invading kingdom which is at war with the world of the enemy. Therefore we should expect opposition and disbelief. We should expect sceptics to remain unconvinced. We should expect life in the overlap to be difficult and signs of the kingdom to be dismissed. Even Jesus' miracles did not convince the sceptical. Instead they exposed their hardness of heart.

Jesus' wonders are always given alongside faith, and his signs of the kingdom are revealed only to those who are hungry for the kingdom of God. Our faith is not founded in signs and wonders – no matter how impressive they are, or how well they fit with modern scientific insights. Rather, signs and wonders are a consequence of faith and are not seen without faith.

Our faith rests securely on the Christian message and on Christ himself. He is the truth incarnate, and all our speaking about miracles is meant to point to him. Our debates about the definition of miracles and our discussions about the intellectual validity of divine healing should not be to prove that *we* are right, but that *he* is right, reliable and true.

Unless our words and actions genuinely point people only to Jesus, we might as well give up. He is the true hope for our hurting world, not us, and people will find healing – lasting, perfect healing – only in him.

# 14

# HEALTHCARE AND HYGIENE

In the last chapter, we noted that the human mind, body and spirit closely interact with each other, and we saw how emotional and spiritual factors can affect our physical bodies. When we go through severe emotional stress, for example, our physical bodies can become ill with a psychosomatic disorder; and if we experience deep inner peace, they can get better. We now need to appreciate that this close interaction also means that the care of our bodies can affect the emotional and spiritual sides of our lives.

We can immediately see that this is true by thinking about the spiritual discipline of fasting. It has been the experience of believers throughout the ages that there are a variety of emotional and spiritual consequences when we add the physical action of refusing to feed our bodies to the spiritual action of praying. The spiritual impact of fasting is only a mystery to those who emphasise the separation of the physical from the spiritual and the emotional.

When Christian believers consider the principles of divine healing, they usually focus on the way that God's Spirit supernaturally intervenes to bring health, healing and wholeness to the human body. We have seen, however, that Christian leaders are increasingly realising that God also heals us immanently through natural, medical and psychological processes, and that we therefore need a broader understanding of divine healing and a wider understanding of the miraculous than has been previously held.

I do not believe that we should stop at this point. Rather, we should move on to recognise the genuine importance of health, hygiene, diet, nutrition and fitness. This emphasis on wholeness is not rooted in my past as a professional dancer – though that does help! – instead it is based firmly on what I read in God's word.

Few modern believers read the books of Leviticus and Deuteronomy for pleasure, yet they contain some remarkable practical guidelines for good health. I doubt whether the nation of Israel would have survived in the wilderness if the Israelites had not lived by their God-given 'sanitary and dietary codes'. Scattered throughout the Pentateuch are rules relating to public hygiene, water supply, sewage disposal, inspection and selection of food, and the control of infectious disease. These holy rules were as binding on the Jews as the Ten Commandments and all the different regulations for worship, sacrifice and sexual behaviour. The Jews had such an integrated view of the human personality that divine dietary requirements were treated in exactly the same way as divine laws about sin offerings, tithes, prayer and priestly behaviour.

The Law of Moses shows us that there is no divide between the sacred and the secular. God is as interested in the way that his people dispose of their sewage as in how they offer him praise; in what they eat as well as how they worship; in holy lives, sane minds *and* healthy bodies. The Old Testament rules show that – no matter what we think or how we live – our spiritual lives are fully integrated with our emotional and physical lives. This means that health is as much an issue of godliness as sexual morality and religious worship; that diet, fitness, exercise and personal hygiene are deeply spiritual issues.

The Mosaic Law went into tremendous detail. It insisted that fruit must not be eaten until a tree was at least five years old. It prescribed herbivores, ruminants and fish as acceptable sources of food. It excluded all birds which lived on animal food, and, among invertebrates, only permitted the eating of locusts. It prohibited the consumption of animals which had died from natural causes – and of the fat and blood from all animals. It laid down special rules for the slaughter and inspection of carcasses to ensure that all meat was free from any taint of infectious disease – there would have been no chance of mad cow disease in Israel! Even the Law's demand for the periodic cleaning out and destruction of leaven was important for maintaining pure food.

God's rules for Israel forbade the sowing of a mixture of seeds at the same time in a field, the growing of crops in a vineyard, the cross-grafting of fruit trees and the cross-breeding of cattle. Regular rest was compulsory for both humans and animals. People suspected of having infectious diseases were isolated. A mixture of wool and linen could not be used in clothing, as this could not be so thoroughly cleaned as a pure garment made from one material. Homes had to be built with parapets to prevent accidents. Excreta had to be buried. People who touched corpses had to clean themselves and their clothes with enormous care. And there were many complicated and detailed rules about washing and purification so that the possibility of passing on an infection was minimised.

As Christians, we know that we no longer have to obey all the details of the Mosaic Law – for Jesus' perfect fulfilment of the Law and the Prophets resulted in a new era in which we can be governed personally by God.

Many believers turn to Moses' Law to emphasise that one or two carefully selected sections must be obeyed today. Most Christians, for example, still think that they have to obey the Ten Commandments to please God. I believe that this is a tragic misuse of the Old Testament. To be consistent, those people who believe that the Law still applies should keep every tiny detail and not pick out a few favourite bits.

Since the death and resurrection of Christ, we do not have to bury our excreta, avoid pork, rest completely every seventh day, keep the Ten Commandments, offer blood sacrifices, and so on, in order to satisfy God. Christian righteousness – life under the personal rule of God – is much simpler than the Law, as God's rule can be summarised in the two simple principles spelt out by Jesus in Matthew 22:37–39.

Christian living is non-legalistic because it is person-centred – because it is a living, personal relationship with Jesus. Matthew 28:18–20 makes it plain that we are to live by his words rather than by the detailed requirements of the Old Testament Law.

We must not forget, however, that Jesus taught that his rule is more radical and demanding than the Law's. Although Christian righteousness does not simplistically continue the details of the Law, all the principles behind the Law are supposed to be fulfilled and exceeded by all disciples. This means that the principles behind the Jewish 'sanitary code' are as important for us today as the principles behind their 'sacrificial code', and that the ideas behind their dietary rules are just as relevant for us as those behind their morality rules.

The Old Testament healthcare and hygiene rules are significant for modern believers in three basic ways, and we need to grasp these if we are to develop an understanding of divine healing which reflects all the biblical emphases.

First, our healing God is deeply interested in so-called practical issues. Health, diet, fitness, hygiene, preventative medicine, the care of those who are highly infectious, even the way we deal with the dead and dying – all of these issues matter to the God who made us as physical beings.

Second, the inclusion of the dietary and sanitary codes in the Mosaic Law shows that we are integrated personalities. The codes indicate that the way we care for our bodies is bound to have a considerable impact on our mental and spiritual health.

Our physical bodies are gifts from God – they were created by him through the process he designed. At the beginning of humanity, he breathed into a body and it became a living human being – an integrated moral, social, spiritual, sexual, sane and physical being. If we follow the Creator's principles we will be healthy and whole in every area of life. And if we disregard any of his principles – in any area of living – we are liable to be affected spiritually, emotionally *and* physically. This is as true in matters like our diet, exercise and rest as it is in our sexual and social behaviour.

And, third, there are practical divine principles which we should follow to stay healthy and whole. The God who made us knows how to maintain us, and in Exodus, Leviticus and Deuteronomy he has given us some natural principles of health. At the most simple level of all, these show that we are far more likely to keep fit, stay healthy and live longer if we eat simply, wash thoroughly, exercise sensibly, rest regularly, and keep away from dirt and infections. But at a deeper and more important level, they show that this works only if the people around us follow similar principles.

The Old Testament rules were given to keep a whole nation healthy. If one person broke the sanitary or dietary code, there were health consequences for all the people around them. According to Jesus, one of the two key principles of the whole Mosaic Law is that we are social beings with a responsibility to love our neighbour as ourselves. This means that the spiritual issues of diet, exercise, rest and cleanliness are not individual issues which people should resolve privately, but are corporate matters which we should consider and apply congregationally.

I find it extraordinary that many leaders who preach divine healing principles in their churches, and encourage their members to pray for healing, do not also teach divine healthcare principles, and do not actively encourage their people to eat more simply, exercise more rigorously, and live in a way which facilitates global health. If we take our Christian calling seriously, we will not be concerned only with our own spiritual needs and with praying for our supernatural healing: we will also live physically in a way which actively brings health and hope to others. The corporate principle behind the Mosaic Law demands that we develop a deep and holy sense of responsibility for the healthcare and hygiene of others.

We saw in an earlier chapter that simple living is as much a context of the Christian healing ministry as evangelism; now we are able to see why. The way we live physically affects other people physically – and we are called to love others as much as we love ourselves. If we do not want other people – or other nations – to dump their waste on our doorsteps, we should not dump ours on theirs. If we do not want other people to eat so much of our food that there is hardly any left for us, then we should not consume vast quantities of theirs. There is something wrong about wanting to preach spiritual truth to people in developing countries – or even to the poor in our own lands – while we carry on living in an unthinking way which reinforces their physical poverty and poor health.

We saw in Part Two that if we are genuinely concerned to partner God in his healing ministry we must recognise that he has a special concern for the poor. They are generally those who have the poorest health, the shortest life expectancy, and the least access to medical resources. The average life expectancy in the Republic of Benin is only forty-seven years and 15 per cent of children die before they reach the age of five. This is mainly because two thirds of the population does not have access to safe water, nearly four million people are without access to health services, and the average calorie consumption for the whole nation is 5 per cent less than the United Nations minimum requirement. And Benin is only a tiny country that most people know little about – there are many other countries in Africa and Asia with much larger populations and far greater health problems.

*O*ur healing God is involved in healing at every level. He has created humanity with bodies which have the capacity for self-healing, and has designed us with an in-built ability to fight disease. He has given men and women creative, enquiring minds which have enabled them to study his creation and to use it and shape it to aid healing through medical and psychological processes. He has provided us with principles to live by which help us to stay healthy and to serve him on earth for the full length of our days. He gave us his redeeming Son so that we can be perfectly healed and can look forward with absolute hope to the day of resurrection when pain, tears, disease and all the other effects of God's curse will cease. And he has anointed his disciples with his Holy Spirit so that we can offer his miraculous healing to the hurting people around us.

Partners in God's healing ministry are called to embrace every aspect of his healing work so that people get the full picture about God, and worship him as Creator *and* Redeemer. Those church leaders who ignore God's general healthcare principles, but urge people to receive his miraculous healing, can hardly complain when other people do the reverse! As Christians, we believe that our bodies are created gifts, which we would do well to look after as we are answerable to God for the way that we use all his gifts. However, we go further than this, for we also believe that our bodies are temples of the Holy Spirit. This means that the way we treat our bodies is one measure of our attitude to God himself. It surely does not honour him if we allow his temple to become a polluted, poisoned, wheezing, over-weight and out-of-condition hulk of flab!

Of course, we need to be careful that we do not become too concerned with healthcare issues and the condition of our bodies. In the past, there have been groups within the Church which over-emphasised asceticism and self-deprivation. Believers became hermits or pillar saints – or fasted excessively and practised self-flagellation – because they believed that punishing the body was the key to developing the spirit. Although few modern British Christians punish their bodies, there are some who are preoccupied with pampering their bodies. They are so interested in the condition or appearance of their bodies that they spend a disproportionate amount of time or money on them to the neglect of the spiritual side of their lives.

Legalism is always lurking in the shadows as a snare for unwary believers, and there are still those who foolishly link their spirituality to a strict regime of dietary laws. Paul deals with this in 1 Corinthians 8, where he shows that food does not commend us to God. We are not spiritually superior because we eat or do not eat particular types of food. God wants us to live by his personal day-to-day directing, not by a list of rules.

It is the same with other healthcare issues like cleanliness, rest and exercise. We are meant to be enslaved only to God and so we should make sure that we do not slip into bondage to particular habits or regimes. The enemy is always trying to trap us into some form of addiction because this means that we are not ruled fully by God. He does not mind whether we are addicted to sport or chocolate, to caffeine or cocaine, to music or clothes, to cars or committee meetings, to alcohol or religion – as long as there is some area of our lives which is not under the exclusive rule of God.

I f we are concerned about the Christian healing ministry, we must be aware of the huge changes in the general attitude to healthcare which have occurred in the last decade.

In western Europe, health is now a booming industry and a tremendous number of companies are trying to exploit current fashions in fitness, hygiene, nutrition, diet, massage, vitamins and alternative remedies. Every section of the media regularly dispenses propaganda which urges us to spend vast sums of money on healthcare and hygiene products.

Today, it is not only Christians who lay hands on the sick, nor is it just doctors who offer prescriptions. A whole host of New Age ideologies and non-Christian philosophies have identified with the current interest in health and are eagerly trying to promote their unbiblical concepts through health products and practices.

Some Christians are alert to this danger, but instead of being discerning and discriminating they have automatically rejected the whole area as demonic. As we have seen, the enemy will always seek to trap us into either addiction or legalism. He is equally delighted when we refuse – without referring to the Spirit and the word – ever to have anything to do with something or become deeply involved. For example, most Christians do not develop the important biblical discipline of meditating on God's word and God's creation because many non-Christian groups use different forms of meditation. And most believers steer away from all alternative or complementary medical remedies simply because they have heard that some practitioners use occult practices in diagnosis.

Christians need to recognise that there has been a considerable shift in attitudes. Many people have turned away from a rationalistic way of thinking and have adopted a more open, 'post-modern' view of life. The age of deference is passing and a new era is beginning where everyone's opinion is equally valid. Ideas are not tested. There are no absolutes and no measures. People want their children to be happy, rather than good. If something seems to work, it is accepted without question. Some of the new studies into behavioural medicine – which we noted in the last chapter – have drawn in 'healers' from a wide variety of 'spiritual' traditions. One recent study of AIDS at the California Pacific Medical Center involved twenty 'faith healers' from Buddhism and Native American traditions praying for patients for an hour a day for ten weeks.

Some Christian believers hoped that this new atmosphere would help the cause of the gospel, but they should have realised that any new secular openness would not embrace biblical Christianity. Whatever the change of climate in the enemy's kingdom, it will always be at war with the kingdom of God.

There are several reasons for this change. Some people became disillusioned with the blatant materialism and consumerism of the eighties and started searching for gentler ways of living. A concern for the environment and 'green issues' has prompted many people to turn to more 'natural' remedies and treatments. Large hospitals have isolated many doctors from their communities, and health reforms have given doctors less time with their patients. This has led many people to feel that medical treatment is not as accessible and available as in the past, and they have started to consider alternatives.

In the early nineties, a friend of mine used to have an office above a 'Complementary Health Centre', and he was amazed at the continuous stream of visitors searching for alternative forms of healthcare. According to him, most of them were bringing their children for 'natural treatment' and 'alternative remedies'. He shared a kitchen and reception area with the Centre and got to know the staff very well. After three years, he concluded that some of the healthcare treatments were surprisingly useful, some were completely crackers, some were downright demonic – and that they were all making an absolute fortune!

The main point we must understand about alternative healthcare treatments is that they claim to heal the whole person. Proponents recognise that the mind, the body and the spirit do form a unity, and they are aiming to affect every aspect of the sick person's life – including the spiritual side. This is what is meant by the expression 'holistic medicine'. The question we should ask ourselves is whether the way that a practitioner or product is seeking to affect the whole person – including the human spirit – is compatible with God's word.

We need to be careful that we do not automatically categorise as demonic things which seem strange just because they are unusual. At the beginning of the twentieth century, many believers dismissed air travel as demonic because some versions of the Bible described Satan as the prince of the power of the air! In this area, as in every aspect of the Christian life, the secret lies in listening carefully to God through the word and the Spirit. I suggest that there are four basic principles which can guide us.

First, we should not be misled by pragmatism. The fact that a treatment or remedy works physically or mentally is not an adequate spiritual justification for its use. The inter-reaction of body, mind and spirit can mean that a physical cure leads to spiritual darkness, or that mental peace leads to spiritual imprisonment. Counterfeit miracles do occur. The deceiver does appear as 'an angel of light'. Pagan supernatural cures do have their origin in something other than the name of Jesus.

Second, we should concentrate more on the means of diagnosis than the method of treatment. We need to find out how information is obtained, and avoid any practitioner who uses an occult means of diagnosis. The Mosaic Law contains clear guidelines about forbidden occult practices – Deuteronomy 18:10–12, for example, shows that we should avoid any contact with the dead or the spirits of the dead. Any healthcare practice or product which refers to spirits other than the Holy Spirit must be avoided, as must those which involve the use of pendulums, pyramids, rods, forces, princes, energies and guides.

Third, we should educate ourselves about the principles behind the different practices. We have seen that western medicine ignores the spiritual side of humanity and asks only *how* questions. Much of alternative healthcare has a different view and is as concerned with *why* questions as we are. But instead of looking to the Bible for answers, it has concluded that sickness is the result of an imbalance of 'energy' levels in the body. This idea comes from ancient Eastern religions which presume that there are two opposing, but balancing, forces in the universe which are also present in the body. When these are imbalanced, the 'life force' or 'vital energy' in the body is disturbed and sickness is the consequence.

The issue for Christians is not whether the different remedies and practices based on this spiritual idea work, but whether

160

the spiritual idea behind them is correct. We are part of one groaning creation, and there are two opposing forces in the universe – but they are not meant to be balanced and they are very far from equal! In fact, our whole calling in life is to trample on the works of the enemy, and to establish the kingdom of God.

Fourth, we should be open to using those healthcare products which are honestly 'natural' and 'herbal', and those practices which are genuinely based in massage and manipulation. If somebody imported the balm of Gilead and marketed it in Britain today it would be an alternative healthcare treatment which many strange groups would probably use. But how could we reject it when it is so highly regarded in the Bible? We should be aware, however, that there are few medical safeguards in this area, that the claims of effectiveness can be over-stated, that the main aim is to make money, and that there may be unfortunate side-effects.

In the end, I do not believe it is a coincidence that all books written by occult practitioners and New Age proponents advocate nearly all the alternative means of healthcare. As Christian believers, we do need to be discerning – and very aware that the way we treat our bodies can have a considerable impact on our spirits and emotions. Instead of running to unknown practices based on pagan views of the world, it is surely much better that we build our lives on godly healthcare principles. If we genuinely want to live for the glory of God, and to be an appropriate temple for the Holy Spirit, we will want to live by such principles, and we will apply them as the Spirit personally directs us.

I believe that there are four simple spiritual principles of health which we need to apply. They are principles, not rules and regulations. They are spiritual principles because they are activated and promoted by or in the Spirit. And they are health principles, because they affect the whole person – body, spirit and mind – and bring health and wholeness to every aspect of the human personality. These four simple principles will help us to stay healthy and whole, but they will not make us more spiritual, or wise, or super-fit Olympians!

As Christians living under the rule of God we know that 'Jesus is Lord'. Every aspect of our whole being is meant to be submitted to, and controlled by, the Lord Jesus through the Holy Spirit. In practice, this means that Jesus is the centre of our lives and we ask him to control everything – our eating and drinking, our exercising and resting, our spending and giving, our thinking and praying.

The first simple principle is that we need to have a balanced diet, good nutrition and a healthy intake of vitamins. God has given us mouths, tongues, taste-buds, stomachs, digestive organs, the sense of smell and the ability to enjoy food. He has made us in such a way that we need to eat healthily and moderately to stay well. Over-eating is just as harmful to health as under-eating – and far more common in western nations. When we think about eating disorders, we tend to focus on helping young women who are preoccupied with becoming thin. I suspect that we also need to concentrate on helping older men and women whose bodies reveal that their eating habits are making them rather unhealthy. Remember, we never see a fat centenarian!

Advertising puts tremendous pressure on us to eat unhealthily. Most food and drink adverts are for products which we would be healthier – and wealthier – without. We all know that chocolates, sweets, crisps, cakes, biscuits and fizzy drinks rot our teeth and – taken in excess – cause obesity and ill health, and that we should consume much more fish, fresh fruit and raw vegetables if we want to be healthy. Advances in nutrition have shown us that we need to eat more fibre, much less fat, as little sugar as possible, and food which contains a balance of vitamins and minerals. Recent studies have shown just how important many vitamins and natural substances are to our health, and we should supplement those which are absent from our diet. These are not secular issues which Christians can be neutral about, they are spiritual issues which determine how useful believers are in the service of God.

This does not mean that unhealthy or sick people are not useful to God, for I know several housebound saints who have developed enormously important ministries of inter-cession. However, over-eating – and addictions to convenience foods and drinks – slashes years off saints' lives and robs God's kingdom of huge amounts of much-needed finance. As little as thirty years ago, the most that the Church ever had to say on this area was, 'Don't smoke and don't drink.' Today, we often say even less. We must not drift back into the legalism of early generations, but the fear of legalism must not stop us from encouraging people to eat and drink in a way which brings health to their lives and makes them more useful to God.

Our all-healing God is gracious, and he is filled with an incredible willingness to heal, but it is rather presumptuous to eat and to drink in a way which we know will eventually make us ill – and to think that we can then beg God to heal us. If there was a heavy smoker in our congregation, would it be right to ignore his addiction and just keep on promising him healing when his lungs finally pack up? It is equally wrong to demand God to heal our clogged arteries, our over-strained hearts and our intestinal disorders, when he has shown us how to eat to prevent these ailments from occurring. Healing grace does abound, but I do not think we should eat to make it abound!

In the Scriptures, there is a pattern of feasting and fasting among God's people. We must not be so preoccupied with being healthy that we never celebrate God's goodness with the occasional gargantuan feast. But, equally, the majority of western believers would benefit physically – let alone spiritually – from regular fasting. When I was working as a dancer, I had to control my diet for the sake of the performance of the whole company. An overweight dancer who ate foolishly and unhealthily would have been thrown out! I am sure that we need such a sense of the Church militant – and of our indispensable part in it – that we are also prepared to control all our bodily urges for the sake of the kingdom.

The second simple principle is that we need to have regular exercise and a good level of fitness. God has made us with muscles which start to atrophy if they are not stretched and strengthened, and with joints which stiffen when they are not used enough. Yet our modern society is increasingly sedentary

– we sit for almost everything and rarely exert ourselves physically.

Centuries ago, no British church buildings had pews or seats and everyone stood throughout the service. This still happens in many less-developed nations. Some Christians mock those who protest when pews are removed from an old church building, but I wonder what they would say if someone threatened to remove their chairs and make them stand for an hour each Sunday! Our forefathers would not have flinched. We are not fit enough to manage it comfortably.

Scientists have shown us that a fit human body not only provides more energy to carry out physical activities, it also means a more alert mind, quicker mental responses, and a significantly increased resistance to disease. The contemporary phrase, 'Use it or lose it' has many different applications in this area. I am sure that the integration of spirit, mind and body means that fitter bodies are also more spiritually attentive, as well as being able to work harder and longer in God's service.

Western doctors agree that most of us do not exercise nearly enough. It seems quite simple to me: if we want to be able to serve God for longer – and at a higher level of usefulness – we will choose to exercise more. But if we are happy with increasing immobility, growing discomfort and fewer years to serve God, we will carry on sitting and getting less and less fit.

It is so straightforward for us all to build simple times of exercise into our daily schedules. Research shows that stretching and strengthening our muscles for thirty minutes a day, five days a week, would transform our health. We could do this by walking or cycling more. We could take up a sport. We could use the stairs instead of the lift or escalator. We could dig our garden and grow lots of healthy fresh vegetables. We could join an exercise class – and so on. It's easy – if we have the will and the motivation!

The bodies that God gave humanity have been designed by him to be maintained through exercise, and we are foolish if we do not maintain them in his way. When we abide by his principles of health, we are more likely to stay healthy; when we do not follow his principles we are vulnerable to disease and accident. I am convinced that it is as irresponsible for God's soldiers to allow the physical condition of their bodies to deteriorate as it is for dancers or athletes to refuse to train properly.

In contrast to the first two principles, the Church has tended to make a great deal of the third simple principle of health. The idea that we need regular rest and relaxation is another theme which runs through creation. Animals have been made with the need for sleep so that they can be refreshed. Plants have a cycle of growth and rest. The 'Sabbath' principle suggests that humans need one day in seven free from work and as different as possible from the other six.

It is obvious that we need regular rest so that we can be refreshed and renewed. And we know that it is not only our bodies which are affected when we sleep badly – our minds and spirits also suffer. But as well as rest, we need relaxation – a change of activity, as well as periods of non-activity.

Some parts of the Church have been keen to impose one form of the Sabbath principle on society, but many of us have missed the principle behind this detail of the Mosaic Law. It is not merely that God is so important that we should set one day a week apart to concentrate on him – for he should be central to every day – it is also that we have been made with the need for one day a week which is quite different from the other six.

If we are to become whole and healthy people, we need to become more 'complete' people with a range of healthy interests. Christians whose lives revolve entirely around their work, their families and their church tend not to be particularly interesting people – and they are usually not that accessible to people who are not yet Christians.

God is essentially a creative creator with a love of endless variety and a predilection for extraordinary detail. This is reflected in humanity, and there is something of God's lavish creativity in each of us. We do have to work. We must care for our families. Christian service and witness should dominate our lives. But if we want to stay sane and healthy we will make time to express God's creativity and to appreciate his creativity in others.

Art, literature, sport, sculpture, music, dance, crafts, hobbies, gardening, all reveal something of God's creativity and we find that we are refreshed by spending time contemplating or participating in these activities. Any Christian involvement in a creative activity helps to bring a degree of godly health and wholeness to our integrated lives, for it refreshes our bodies, satisfies our minds, and stimulates our spirits.

The fourth simple health principle is that we need to exercise our minds, and express our emotions. Psychosomatic medicine has shown us the extent to which our lives are affected by emotional stress and mental pressure. The Bible teaches that our behaviour is controlled by our thinking, and urges us to think like God and to be renewed in our thinking by him. When we think God's way, we live God's way, and we experience his wholeness and health.

If we want to be healthy, we must recognise that it is not enough to eat healthily, exercise vigorously and rest regularly – we also need emotional stability and mental activity. Interestingly, a recent study of nuns' brains shed new light into the prevention of Alzheimer's disease. One order had, over several years, allowed scientists to examine their brains after death. The researchers were surprised to discover that many of the brains had been badly affected by Alzheimer's, but that the nuns had not exhibited any of the symptoms of the disorder in their lives. These nuns were those who had been the most mentally active from youth, reading regularly, doing crosswords, struggling with ideas, and so on. It seems that their long years of mental activity and agility had an unforeseen health consequence. This suggests that regular mental activity is as important for good health as regular physical activity. The phrase, 'use it or lose it' applies as much to the mind as to the body!

God has made us as rational and emotional beings. Many people today suggest that we are either ruled by our 'heads' – our minds – or by our 'hearts' – our emotions. However, it is important to recognise that the Bible teaches that our minds affect and determine everything. Our emotions are merely by-products which stem from our thinking, culture and behaviour, they are simply the result of the way that we view things. Emotions – feelings – are indicators which enhance our lives by adding colour, passion, warmth and self-expression, and which damage our health when they are repressed. But we are conditioned by our minds, by what we think.

God has made us to be controlled by sane, healthy minds, so the enemy ruthlessly targets our thinking. Just as he pressurises us to eat badly, to exercise too little and to relax as infrequently as possible, so he uses every possible influence to corrupt our thinking and disrupt our emotions.

The Bible urges us to be renewed in our minds and to be like Christ Jesus in our thinking – this is the godly way to a healthy mind. We can develop a positive, godly mind-set through studying the Scriptures, through gazing at the Gospels, and through fellowshipping with the Spirit. We can develop a positive self-image by seeing ourselves in Christ and appreciating our status in him. This is not a human technique, it is the work of the Spirit in us.

God's way of thinking lifts, builds and strengthens us. It reduces fear, anxiety, anger, resentment and that terrible sense of helplessness and hopelessness which afflicts many people today – and, therefore, it helps to prevent disease and hasten recovery. Good doctrine, the Sermon on the Mount, the Psalms, Paul's letters – these are all vital medicine for the mind and the spirit, and they bring health and wholeness to every aspect of our lives.

While rightly recognising the primacy of the mind, some Christians have mistakenly suggested that emotionalism is some sort of arch sin. Emotions have been devalued in many parts of the Church and – consequently – some believers deny their feelings and are not in touch with their emotions. But repressing emotions creates stress, and that is a sure way to ill-health. God has given us emotions, so we should acknowledge that they have meaning, and we should express and develop them. But, equally, we must resist the modern trend towards subjectivity and feelings-determined behaviour. We are likely to get into difficulties if we follow our feelings, but repressing them, or expressing them without control, are not Christian solutions.

I believe that these four simple, spiritual principles for godly healthcare should be part of the modern Christian healing ministry. As anointed believers, we are not simply spiritual versions of ambulance men, rushing to bring supernatural healing wherever we are directed by our controller. We are also teachers, advisers, counsellors, who gently guide people into and towards God's health and wholeness.

We have been called to bring hope to a hurting world, and God wants us to help people to become whole in every area of their lives. In the Old Testament, for Moses, this meant teaching a mixture of dietary and sanitary rules *and* seeing God heal supernaturally. In the New Testament, for Paul, it meant moving in dynamic signs and wonders *and* advising Timothy to drink wine for the sake of his health. And today, for us, it means that we begin to minister God's supernatural healing *and* to teach his healthcare principles – and to live by them ourselves.

# Part Four

## LOOKING FORWARD

# 15

# DIVINE HEALING TODAY

*A*t most small public events in Britain, there are usually a couple of keen first-aiders wandering around. It is easy to spot them because they wear some kind of drab uniform, carry a pack which looks as though it has not been opened in years, and are commonly accompanied by a pasty-looking teenager with a glazed stare.

I am sure that they could do a wonderful job in an emergency, but they rarely look alert or attractive – and they don't inspire confidence. First aid is merely their hobby, and they give the impression that they are hanging about hoping that someone will trip over and ask for their ministrations. Yet most of the crowd are praying, 'Dear God, if I do have an accident, please make sure that a proper paramedic gets to me first!'

That is probably a dreadful slur on a fine body of people, but it is an uncannily accurate picture of the public's perception of the Christian healing ministry in Britain today. Sadly, we are caricatured as rather extreme, not very bright, incredibly out-of-date, and best avoided. We are widely thought of as socially embarrassing, intellectually inept, and just about as useful as a concrete parachute. According to the media, normal people visit their GPs, only a religious nutcase asks someone like me to pray for them. How Yahweh Rapha must weep!

I t seems to me that we have allowed the sceptical community – in the rationalist, the post-modernist *and* the religious camps – to silence our forthright proclamation of the healing God, to sidetrack us into a less-than-complete idea of divine

171

healing, and to seduce us into thinking that the cause of Christian mission is best served by a marginalisation of the miraculous.

We have been deceived by the ancient lie that a de-supernaturalised Christianity is more likely to be believed by the masses. Yet our world knows that there is nothing worth believing in a miracle-free faith, and people are turning in droves to a pagan mysticism which is rooted in supernatural deception.

We have forgotten that healing miracles are essentially signs pointing to the living God, to the cross and the hope of his glorious kingdom; and we have not recognised that a basic defensive measure of any invaded nation is to destroy all the signposts. The opposition to divine healing in western Europe and the United States is not a measured intellectual response by impartial, caring observers – it is a frantic spiritual attack urged by forces which are implacably opposed to the healing God.

If healing miracles are at the heart of God's self-revealed nature, and are part of the whole scriptural revelation of God's activities, and are evidenced throughout history, we can be certain that it is possible to speak about them with tremendous intellectual and spiritual integrity. However, the backdrop of the wider spiritual battle means that we will be violently opposed – even when our arguments are intellectually convincing, our exegesis is theologically faultless and our healings are medically verified. In fact, we can anticipate that the clearer and more numerous the signs, the greater and more extreme the opposition.

We live in a world which is full of hurting people, of people who are hoping for healing at some level of their being but who are not quite certain where to turn. We need to make it abundantly clear that Yahweh Rapha is deeply concerned about them – about them individually – and that he is willing and able to heal their hurts because he loves them with an inexhaustible passion.

Somehow we have to take healing out of our meetings and into the market place, out of our services and into people's sitting rooms. We need to show the world that divine healing is not something which we hide away at the end of our Christian gatherings, but that it permeates every aspect of life.

We have to keep on making it plain that the divine healing ministry is not only about occasional, inexplicable dramatic miracles when God intervenes supernaturally, but that it is also about frequent, ordinary, ambiguous, partial improvements when God works immanently through natural processes. I am sure that many more believers will understand their calling to be involved as God's partner in supernatural healing when they appreciate that it is a facet of God's healing ministry rather than the totality.

We need to emphasise relentlessly that divine healing is not a tiny fringe activity but a major part of the Church's life. We need to explain that supernatural healing is only one section of the healing ministry, and that the other parts are equally important – that Jesus came as much to heal the broken-hearted as to heal the blind, and Britain has many more people suffering from broken hearts than blind eyes.

The modern plague of divorce has caused an unprecedented level of social isolation and family disintegration, and the Church needs to be a therapeutic community where people know that they will find acceptance, forgiveness, companionship, emotional relief and hope for some sort of future in this life. It is pointless to concentrate on offering a wonderful cure for blindness when the people around us are suffering from aching hearts.

Equally, demographic changes in western society mean that there are larger numbers than ever before of lonely and struggling elderly people. For generations, churches have concentrated on establishing specialist youth ministries and financing youth workers. It cannot be long before we start setting up 'Methuselah' ministries and focus on responding to the special needs of the elderly. God is as interested in healing them as the young and the middle-aged, and the divine healing ministry is obviously particularly relevant for older people. I find it sad when the Church's ministry to the elderly revolves around hymns and sandwiches, when they are usually the ones in most pain and are most aware of their proximity to eternity.

It may not be appropriate to stress the scriptural emphasis on the divine healing of infertility, but the news that God heals aching joints, improves deaf ears and clears misty eyes and minds is very welcome. All the divine promises about the final transformation are particularly important to the elderly, and we need to help them embrace the promises which God has given and prepare for their own death.

We must continually point out that divine healing is not in opposition to medical healing, and we should clearly support and encourage our own local hospitals and GPs. Prayer for the sick does not only mean asking God for a miracle, it also means asking God to guide, bless and strengthen doctors, dentists, nurses and auxiliary workers. Believers who are professional medical workers need to appreciate that they are a genuine part of the Church's healing ministry. They should grasp that they are as active in passing on God's healing when they are dealing with patients in the course of their work, as when others are ministering powerful signs and wonders at a meeting.

And we must go on teaching and applying biblical healthcare principles. We must encourage people to experience God's gift of health as well as his gift of healing, and show them how to live by his principles. Once preventative healthcare has been given its rightful place in divine healing, I am sure that an unfit, overweight minister will seem just as incongruous as one who smokes.

However, the devil is as delighted when we ignore the supernatural aspect of divine healing as when we focus on it to the exclusion of everything else. The divine healing ministry does involve visiting the ill, washing the sick, comforting the bereaved, stimulating the bored, emptying bottles, encouraging doctors, teaching others to eat and exercise properly, and so on. These are all vital acts of Christian service. The gifts of our time and attention, our words and gestures, our prayers and practical caring all have genuine healing value. But they are not signs, and they are not wonders.

The enemy is opposed to every aspect of healing because he rejoices in suffering and sickness and because he feeds on the emotions they arouse. But he especially resists the supernatural dimension of divine healing because more than anything else it is a sign which points people to the living God, reminds them of the atoning cross, and offers a foretaste of the devil's destruction at the final day.

It is my firm belief that the divine healing ministry – including supernatural signs and wonders – is now open to every Christian believer. In Part Two, we saw that in the Old Testament, only those select few who were anointed with the Holy Spirit – the prophets – were eligible for the healing ministry. But since Jesus baptised the Church in the Holy Spirit at Pentecost, the healing ministry has been a possibility for all believers, whether male or female, black or white, Jew or Gentile, old or young. The only requirement is that the believer has been anointed with the Holy Spirit.

In Matthew 28:18–20, Jesus commissioned the disciples with these words: 'All authority has been given to me in heaven and earth. Go therefore and make disciples of all the nations, baptising them in the name of the Father and of the Son and of the Holy Spirit, teaching them to observe all things that I have commanded you.' This surely means that, right to the end of time, *all* believers in *every* nation are to be taught to obey *all* the instructions which Christ gave to his original twelve apostles. If words mean anything, this must include the evangelistic commission to heal the sick.

Some of us will be more involved in healing than others. A few believers may receive a particular gift of healing. But I know that every single member of God's prophetic people can be his partner in healing. As we have seen, this means that we should avoid styles of ministry which give the impression that only the leaders, or a special few at the front, can bring Christ's healing. We need to minister in an inclusive way which encourages every believer to volunteer as an active healing partner for God.

In writing about prophecy, Paul says – in Romans 12:6 – that those who have received the gift should use it in proportion to their faith. This suggests that the gift can be more or less strongly developed in different people, or in the same person over a period of time. I believe that this is why Paul can remind Timothy, in 1 Timothy 4:14, not to neglect his gift and – in 2 Timothy 1:6 – to rekindle the gift within him.

If it was possible for Timothy to allow his gift to weaken, perhaps through infrequent use, so it is surely similar for us in relation to healing. And if Timothy's gift can be strengthened by using it, so we need to develop all the spiritual and practical skills necessary to partner God effectively in healing.

Since Pentecost, it has been the function of the whole Church – of every individual member – to reveal God's glory in and to the world. This means that – together with the other believers in your area – *you* have been chosen to reveal Yahweh Rapha's healing character to the people in your neighbourhood, to show them the depth of God's love and compassion.

You can be God's partner in healing. In fact, you are meant to be his partner in supernatural healing. You can do this only in and with the Spirit. But you can do it. You can partner God in healing and see him heal the sick. You can make a genuine and tangible difference to the lives of the hurting people around you. Through the Spirit, Jesus is addressing and approaching you. He is urging you into action – to heal the broken-hearted, to comfort the bereaved, to visit the dying, to cure the sick and suffering, to go about doing whatever he directs.

I believe that it is time for us all to move forward in healing. We need to start to grow in faith and in our understanding of the Father's willingness to heal. We need to begin to challenge our own faith. Western society is geared to what can be seen and touched, not to what is written in the word of God and to what is invisible – so we must constantly re-educate ourselves through reading the word.

In particular, we need to gain experience and expertise in the spiritual gifts which are important in ministering healing with God. We know that Jesus heals, and that the Spirit is in us and with us to heal, but we need to grasp the 'how to' of ministering in healing.

Rather than falling into the error of 'demandingness', we must go on trusting God and deepening our relationship with him – even when there is no outward evidence of healing. The most powerful manifestations of healing occur when we realise that we are nothing, so something is terribly wrong if our ministry activity does not deepen our dependence on Christ and our relationship with him.

The time has come for us to believe the word of God rather than our human experience, and to start taking risks for God – to be ready to appear foolish for him. As you approach the end of this book, I ask you to fill yourself with a holy determination to pray for people to be healed. Whatever you may feel like, the truth is that you are free to experiment, to be bold, to make mistakes, to speak and to pray in a way which guarantees that you will look ridiculous unless God honours your words.

I beg you – for the sake of the hurting world and the holy name of God – please summon up the spiritual resolve to give it everything you have! Unless you start to move with the Spirit in healing, you cannot imagine how seriously God will take your intent, or how effectively he will work with and through you.

# 16

# SENSING THE SPIRIT

As far as I am concerned, the whole healing ministry hinges on recognising the promptings and directings of the Spirit. We can know all the theory, recite all the biblical promises, be filled with godly enthusiasm and holy compassion, but we will see nothing happen until we can recognise the way that God communicates with us through the Spirit.

I expect that we have all had spiritual ideas or thoughts or dreams which we have not known what to do with. In Part One, I related how, as a young man, I sensed that a woman would be sitting in a particular seat in a church I was visiting. She turned out to be blind, but I did not know what to do with the information I had received – so I failed God and I failed the woman.

After helping thousands of people to begin partnering God in healing, I now know that almost every believer has sensed that God has wanted them to do something or say something to a sick person. But they too have not known what to do with the impression and so have done nothing.

God's earliest anointed partners in healing, the Old Testament prophets, were inspired to speak and to act both by the word of God and by the Spirit of God – and I believe that we can expect to be directed in a similar way. Some prophets, Moses, for example, were principally 'word inspired' prophets and others, like Elijah, were more 'Spirit inspired', but we should not make too much of the distinction.

I cannot read the Old Testament without being amazed at the dynamic impact of the word of the Lord upon the prophets.

Amos 3:8 reports, 'The Lord God has spoken! Who can but prophesy?' And when you recognise God's voice in a similar clear way, I am sure that you will respond in the same fashion.

'The word of the Lord came to' is the scriptural phrase which usually describes this mode of inspiration, but I think that 'came to' is better translated as either 'became actively present to' or, more simply, 'was to'. This seems to describe an internal awareness of God's message which grows over a period of time. In Zechariah 1:1, it developed over a period of a month, though sometimes the inspiration was more immediate, as in Zechariah 1:7. On other occasions, this internal prompting of the prophets stemmed from events as ordinary as the sight of an almond tree, two baskets of figs, or a visit to a local factory or building site.

In these instances, God passed on his promptings in the intimacy of private fellowship with the prophet, rather than with a sudden flash of illumination when the prophet was about to minister. This is inspiration or ministry direction as the result of meditation, reflection, observation and study.

In recent years, there has been such an emphasis on 'spontaneity' that many believers expect God to speak to them only at the last second. But, very often, his prompting will develop or grow as we study and read his word, or when we are pondering his thoughts.

A sense of the miraculous sometimes develops in my spirit when I am praying at home, and I gradually become sure that God wants to heal in some way at some point in the near future. I find that I have to strain my 'ears' for the slightest prompting, for the merest whisper of a sense of direction. God does not shout at us with an audible voice. Instead, he speaks with a still, small voice, and we will miss him if we are not paying close attention. For myself, I 'hear' his voice as a gentle hint or a quiet sensing. It is never more than an impression, and I have had to learn to trust and to act upon these thoughts.

Habakkuk 1:1 refers to the 'burden' of the Lord. Some translations render this as 'message' or 'oracle', but literally it means a load or burden – rather like a heavy rucksack. The phrase conjures up a picture of God allowing his anointed partner to feel what he feels about a situation. Isaiah often describes feeling the burden of the Lord about other nations, and Jeremiah identified false prophets as his burden from the Lord. Again, this appears to describe a growing awareness rather than a sudden flash of inspiration.

It may well be that we hear about a person suffering from a particular ailment, and find ourselves moved with extraordinary compassion – something well beyond our normal level of concern. Then, as time goes by, we find that this particular ailment keeps on cropping up: we read a newspaper article about it, somebody refers to it, and so on. Gradually we develop a real burden for that ailment.

It may be that God wants us only to pray for a particular person who is suffering from that condition. But it is far more likely that God has given us his burden so that we will partner him in healing someone from the ailment. When we have such a burden, we need to ask God what he wants us to do with it, and what he is going to do through it. I guarantee that the time will come when the burden has to be discharged, and God will expect us to minister to a person with the ailment. Do not be surprised to come across someone with the condition you are concerned about in the train, at a party, in a supermarket, or even in a meeting!

The Scriptures teach such a real association between receiving the Spirit and speaking God's words that it can never be overstated. Numbers 11:29 is the first hint of a link between them. The experiences of Saul in 1 Samuel 10 and 1 Samuel 19:18–24 show that the anointing of the Spirit in the Old Testament led to spontaneous prophecy. Joel 2:28 makes it clear that receiving the Spirit should result in the activity of speaking God's thoughts or words. This is instant inspiration for immediate delivery.

God does often speak to us quietly over a period of time, preparing us so that we are ready to work with him. But he also speaks to us when he wants us to minister, and this is generally through what has come to be known as 'words of knowledge'.

In the New Testament, we often see Jesus and the early

church leaders sensing that God wanted them to minister to a particular person, and, with the Spirit's help, they identified that person in a crowd. For example, Jesus healed only one man at the pool of Bethesda, and Peter and John knew that God wanted them to heal the lame man at the crowded Temple gate.

For myself, when I am aware in my spirit that God is healing people, or is about to heal people, I will often sense some sort of description of either the person or the condition he is going to heal. At times, I will have a visual impression of the person, and will 'see', for example, a middle-aged woman dressed as a nurse sitting in a wheelchair. On other occasions, I may 'feel' a pain or warmth or tingling or discomfort in part of my own body, and I now recognise that this is one of the Spirit's ways of indicating to me that he is healing a condition in that part of the body.

As well as being directed by God in these ways, the Old Testament prophets also laid claim to frequent inspiration through visions by day and dreams by night. Numbers 12:6 establishes the principle, and Isaiah 6, Ezekiel 12:27, Daniel 7:1 and Zechariah 1:8 demonstrate the practice. It is not a common occurrence for me, but I have been woken several times during the night to realise that God has been speaking to me through a dream, showing me what he is going to do.

During the last ten years, I have slowly begun to recognise the Spirit's promptings and to trust him more and more. I have learnt – through many mistakes and disappointments – how important it is to wait for the Spirit, instead of dashing ahead in human enthusiasm or because of people's expectations.

Whenever I sense that I am being prompted to minister – whether in public or private, at a service or in the street – I find that there are three critical questions which I need to answer. 'Am I hearing the Spirit correctly?' 'Have I the faith and bravery to rise to the challenge?' 'Am I courageous enough to wait for the Spirit and not to fake anything?'

When I am doing everyday things like travelling and shopping, the greatest temptation for me is to do nothing. If I hear the Spirit prompting me to pray for a stranger, I soon hear the enemy urging me not to make a fool of myself, not to embarrass the person, not to risk making a mistake. And when I am speaking at a meeting, he pressurises me not to disappoint the people who want a good show! I have been tempted to speak vague and general words rather than to wait for the Spirit's specific word for a particular person.

It is a basic principle of ministry that God does not give power for what he is not doing, but that he always provides power for what he is doing. Some people appear to think that God gives us unlimited power, and that – once we have received his healing anointing with the Spirit – we should be able to minister powerfully whenever and wherever we are. Yet we know that Jesus, who was fully God and – as a man – had been anointed with the Spirit without measure, did not heal everyone. We have seen how Jesus healed all those who were brought to him, and that he took God's healing directly to specific individuals – ignoring crowds of other sick people around them. Clearly, he did only what the Father was doing; he stuck rigidly to the Spirit's agenda.

We are doomed to disappointment and embarrassing failure if we try to take the lead in ministry or follow our own inclination. It is vital that we wait for the Holy Spirit and receive specific directions and revelation from him before we proceed in active ministry.

Most believers find that knowing God's will is one of the hardest parts of the Christian life. We all long to obey him – we know that is the best thing to do – but we do not always know what he wants us to do. Instead of waiting for direction, we presume and flounder around, doing whatever seems to be best.

In John 10:16 and 27, Jesus promised that his sheep would hear his voice. This is a promise which he has kept. By the Spirit, we do hear Christ's voice. The problem is that even some believers who have been Christians for many years still do not recognise his voice when they hear it.

Sometimes we hear his voice, but we are not sure whether it really is his voice, or our own thoughts or demonic temptations. At other times, our minds are so full of clutter and distractions that we cannot hear his voice clearly. We know that he is speaking to us, but we cannot make out what he is saying.

I have found that – for me – it is vital to spend time waiting on God before I begin listening to God. If I start asking the Spirit questions too soon, my mind is too busy and noisy to hear his quiet replies. I have found that I need to wait patiently on God – creating an oasis of peace in my life through meditating on the word – before I start listening for the Spirit's direction. I need to make sure that I am alone and free from all possible distractions. Ideally, I try to ensure that I still myself by quietly reading the Scriptures for about an hour. Next, I spend time dealing with my feelings of anxiety and worthlessness – allowing the love of God to drive out all my fears. Only then am I ready to 'tune in to the Spirit' and receive his directions.

I expect that we all need to spend far more time in listening prayer than we do, as most of our times of prayer tend to be mainly one way. We spend time asking God to do things, rather than asking him what we should do and listening for his reply. Asking God specific questions is probably the best way of learning to identify God's voice. We must not be frightened to ask God what we should do or say. But we must remember to make sure that we take note of any thoughts which come into our minds – and that we put those thoughts into practice and see what happens!

We will learn to recognise God's quiet voice only when we act on what we hear in our inner spirits. Some people are so worried about doing something wrong that they never do anything, whereas others are so confident that every crazy thought is a divine instruction that they say and do ridiculous things. This means that we need to exercise discernment when we listen for God's answers to our questions.

God does not promise us sensational results if we do what he says, and he does not try to persuade us to do something by telling us what our obedience will achieve. That is a worldly way of thinking. Equally, God never asks us to do something which is contrary to the Scriptures, or which is destructive or lacking in love. Instead, his thoughts always encourage, build, mend and comfort.

When the Spirit prompts, he simply tells us what to do, without any reasons or explanations, because he wants to develop our faith and trust. Then he gently persists with that same thought over a period of time.

As time goes by, we do begin to recognise the Spirit's special way of speaking to us – but we should never stop spending time alone with him to develop our relationship. We will also increasingly recognise his way of interrupting our thoughts when he wants us to speak to, or minister to, a particular person. I find that many of the most precious times of healing ministry occur when I trust these sudden, unsought thoughts.

By now, I hope you are convinced that God is concerned for his Church to become a genuine healing community which ministers healing in the broadest possible way. I trust you also realise that divine healing does not only mean sensational miracles, so please expect the Spirit to guide you in a whole host of healing activities.

Living in partnership with the Spirit means being ready to be involved in anything on his healing agenda – small, unseen words and deeds of comfort, as well as more public signs and wonders. He is as likely to prompt you to take some flowers to a lonely person as to pray for the healing of someone who is dying from cancer. This means we must not ignore the 'everyday' thoughts that the Spirit places in our minds; instead, we should respond to them and use them to develop our understanding of his voice.

God wants to develop his precious relationship with each of us, and to trust us with ever greater things. For most believers, the healing ministry does begin in small ways, and then it develops as we show God that we are ready to respond to his promptings with boldness and obedience.

# 17

# PARTNERING GOD

In this chapter, I am concerned to make some practical suggestions about our involvement in God's healing ministry. They are based on my personal experience of partnering God in healing and on the way that we have developed the healing ministry at Kensington Temple by training our members. The suggestions that I make are not rules for you slavishly to follow, but are guidelines which you should ask the Spirit to interpret and apply to your situation.

We all know that we need to pray more, yet still we pray so little – and I believe that a lack of adequate preparatory prayer is one of the main reasons for the ineffectiveness of so much contemporary ministry. My rough guide is that, perhaps, at least an equal amount of time should be spent in prayer as we anticipate spending in healing ministry. This prayer should feature intercession for boldness, along the lines of Acts 4:29–30, and silent listening when we wait for God's prompting about ministry. Many believers find it helpful to add fasting to their prayers. Those of us who are serious about better healthcare, a simpler lifestyle, and the healing ministry, will not neglect this discipline.

We saw in the last chapter that asking God specific questions is a most helpful feature of preparatory praying. Uncertainty is a greater problem for most of us than disobedience and we learn to recognise God's voice by asking him questions and sensing his replies in our spirits. As we pray, we need to ask God what he is doing and what part he wants us to play. If we are praying about a particular person, we can ask the Father what the real problem is – whether it is physical, emotional, spiritual, demonic or a curse. Most important of all, we can ask God whether his solution is prayer, deliverance, repentance, patience or healing ministry.

*A* s we have seen, the principle of partnership in ministry runs through the Bible. Jesus sent his followers to heal and preach in pairs. One individual alone cannot reflect the image of the triune God; it needs a relationship. The promises of Matthew 18:19–20 are made to two or three, not to one. Protection from the enemy forces is granted to the whole Church, not isolated individuals. All these examples suggest that it should be commonplace to minister healing in pairs or a team, and more unusual to minister singly. The disciples learnt from being with Jesus when he healed, so it is good preparation and training for us to join with another believer who is more experienced. We have found at Kensington Temple that this is a good way to multiply the numbers of our members involved in healing.

There are many advantages when we minister in pairs. There is a geometrical advance in power, protection for each other from mistakes, and a double channel for God to use in communication. Faith is maintained more easily. Courage exists that one person never has. The flow of ministry can pass from one to another as common sense directs. Members of a healing team are precluded from claiming God's work as their own personal achievement. And the inevitable failures are shared.

I think that it is best to avoid having more than three people ministering to one person, as this can be confusing, both for those ministering and the one being healed. Other members of the team who are eager to be involved can sit quietly and unobtrusively while engaging in urgent prayer for the empowering and guidance of those who are ministering.

I find that anointed believers who minister Christ's healing need a very large supply of patience, as resources are quickly drained by delays, problems and difficult, unlovable people. Interestingly, the Bible uses different Greek and Hebrew words for patience towards people and for patience towards circumstances, and it teaches different things about them.

According to the Scriptures, we do not need to pray for patience towards people as we already have Jesus' patience within us. Galatians 3:27 shows that in baptism we were clothed with his garments, and Colossians 3:12 indicates that this includes his patience towards people. This develops within us as one aspect of the Spirit's fruit in our lives. We need this type of patience when people seek ministry at unsocial hours, or when they are shy, nervous and embarrassed, or rude and rejecting, or difficult and demanding. Quite often, our gift to them of Christ's patience is part of their cure.

The Scriptures suggest, however, that we must pray for patience towards circumstances as this is not a free gift which accompanies conversion. We should not seek for our own patience to grow, but rather for it to be replaced by the patience with which Jesus endured the cross. God slowly develops this in us through our testing, training and suffering – and by giving it to those believers who have stretched their personal resources to the limit. We need this type of patience to stop circumstances from dictating our response, and to help us to persevere when discouragement comes and to keep pressing on to complete results.

The healing ministry does not consist only of the recitation of God's words, but is also the radiation of his love – and we need to be thoroughly prepared with both aspects of Christ's patience if we are to do this.

Some believers are attracted to the Christian healing ministry for entirely the wrong reasons. Compassion and obedience motivated Christ. We will have been sidetracked by the enemy if we hope to ogle at a miracle or be entertained by a bodily reaction. And we will have been diverted by the devil if we hope to send out glowing press reports on what has happened among *us* at *our* meetings. We should seek the humble, self-effacing anonymity of the Holy Spirit, and aim to focus all attention upon God, without basking in any associated glory.

We must remember that no human being can ever heal another. The most that we can aim for is to be an unprofitable servant whom God 'tips off' a few minutes in advance of a miracle. Humility is much easier when we have grasped this simple spiritual principle.

The Spirit's main work is to glorify, or illuminate the Son. When an ancient building is floodlit, it is the building which is admired: the floodlight and rays are necessary, but unnoticed. In a healing miracle, the Holy Spirit acts as a floodlight, and our anointed words and actions are like rays of light which emanate from, and are energised by, him. Jesus is the one who is illuminated and glorified. He is the one to whom the healing signs point. He is to be admired, not ourselves or the mighty deeds. Pride has caused the sad downfall of several notable men and women whom God has used greatly in this ministry.

In Part Two of this book, we noticed how the initiative for healing ministry in the Scriptures was usually by either someone requesting, 'Please heal me,' or by God commanding, 'Go and announce my healing to that person.' The split in the New Testament healing miracles is surprisingly exact: half are in response to a divine instruction and half to a human request. I think that each of us should aim for a similar balance in our ministries.

In ministry, we need to listen both to God and to the person we are seeking to help, and this is facilitated by creating a climate of quiet and privacy. Time and again, the Gospels show how Jesus silenced noise or moved into a private place before commencing ministry. We do well when we follow his example.

Jesus did not function only at a supernatural level, but also at the natural level of observation and deduction. Mark 5:9, 8:22–26, 9:14–29, Luke 18:40–43, and John 5:6 report him asking five obvious questions. If he, in his humanity, sometimes needed to ask these questions, then so – sometimes – will we.

1. 'What is your name?' I know that Jesus addressed this question to a demon, but for us it is an important and natural opening question to put to people we do not know. The exchange of names is more than mere politeness for it helps to ensure that our ministry is personal and loving.

2. 'What do you want me to do?' For us, this is better

expressed by, 'What do you want Jesus to do?' This is an important question as it helps the person to be specific and clear.

3. 'Do you want to be well?' It is helpful to make certain that the person really is serious, and aware of the consequences of being healed. We must be sure that we are not trying to 'force' healing on someone. We need to be particularly sensitive in the way we approach those who appear to be physically disabled, and not assume we know what they want God to do.

4. 'How long has this been happening?' Occasionally the circumstances and background of the problem need to be investigated to clarify the cause of the sickness.

5. 'Can you see?' We should always try to establish what has happened during the ministry. It is rather irresponsible to lay hands on one person and then pass quickly on to the next. Of course, we do not need to know all the medical details, for we are not operating as doctors. This also applies to those who professionally are doctors or nurses but who are ministering supernaturally under the Spirit's anointing. We only need to know in what way the person is suffering. We should not focus on the gravity of the problem but rather on the greatness of God.

As well as questioning the person, it is always necessary to ask God whether anything else needs to be known. He may give us a picture or word to pass on, suggest a statement to make, put a question into our mind, or draw our attention to a non-physical cause. If God tells us nothing, this means that the person has told us everything we need to know.

In the Scriptures, the physical conditions of Abimelech, Miriam, Malchus, the man at the pool of Bethesda and the man let down through the roof appear to have had their origin in sin – sin committed either by or against the individual. Some leaders today would demand that Malchus forgive Peter before admitting any possibility of healing his severed right ear, but Jesus was silent about this and healed him unconditionally. Jesus did not insist on a lengthy confession from the man at the pool of Bethesda; instead, he returned *after* the healing to urge the man not to sin any more. At times, as James 5:16 makes plain, there is an association between the confession of sin and the cure, but this is not always the case.

Other leaders teach that a demon lies behind every disease, and demand that a demon is cast out before healing can begin. The Scriptures, however, clearly distinguish between deliverance from evil powers and physical healing, and this difference needs constant emphasis. Casting out demons and healing the sick are two distinct activities. For example, in Luke 13:10, Jesus cast out an evil spirit, and then followed that by touching the woman to heal her bent back. Of course, a person may be healed as a direct consequence of the expulsion of an evil power – as in Matthew 9:32–34 and 12:22 – but we should not build a general principle from these isolated instances. Jesus usually cured people without any reference to specific demonic presence or activity.

There is a natural tendency in all of us to drift into habitual patterns of ministry. Jesus, however, was unpredictable. He did only what the Father told him and his instructions varied with every individual. In Part Two, we noted the many different healing actions used by Jesus and the early Church, and we would do well to follow their example of obedient variety and creativity.

I think, however, that we should appreciate three general scriptural points. Throughout the Bible, when healing, God's servants seem generally to lay their hands on the affected part of the body rather than the top of the head. Second, in the Scriptures, prayer for healing usually takes place before ministry: words of announcement or command, not words of petition or request, accompany biblical healing ministry. Third, as in the cures of Naaman, Miriam and the John 9 beggar, God may prompt us to suggest an action or task for the person to perform – and the healing will normally be delayed until this has been completed.

I make the following suggestions for those believers who are inexperienced in the healing ministry. Please vary them as the Holy Spirit guides you along his own creative path of action.

1. Show Christ's love at all times. Smile, use first names and relax, for God will perform the miracle, not you.

2. Together with your partner, quietly confess and ask

forgiveness of your sins. God rarely works through dirty channels.

3. Ask the Holy Spirit to give you guidance, boldness and power.

4. Keep your eyes open – you are not praying! I do not think that Jesus ministered through locked eyelids, and we often receive helpful information by watching the person's reactions.

5. Listen to God and speak whatever you sense him putting into your mind. He may tell you to command a parasitic growth to be removed, or a defective organ to be restored. He may ask you to give a pronouncement of faith or blessing. Keep on asking God questions and listening to his replies.

6. Ask God whether you should touch the person or not. If you are prompted, gently place your hands on the clothing or skin nearest to the affected part of the body.

7. Ask questions like, 'Do you feel anything?' and, 'What's happening?' Ensure that you are kept informed of the healing progress.

8. Watch out for bodily reactions – shaking, stiffening, variation in breathing, falling or sagging, warmth, tingling, hot spots, laughter, weeping, moist eyes, and so on. Though these reactions may indicate that God is at work, they are only the body's natural response to God's work. They are not in themselves a supernatural work of God. An extreme bodily reaction does not evidence a greater work of God, nor does the absence of any reaction mean that healing is not occurring. These phenomena are no yardstick of progress or effectiveness. Fifty sunbathers lying on a beach for the same length of time will all have different bodily reactions to the sun. It is the same when the Spirit moves in power. A few people always fall over, some shake, others laugh or weep. But many people – as in the gospel stories – do not react bodily.

If a bodily reaction does take place, help the person to be comfortable, but ignore the reaction and press on with the ministry. The reaction sometimes ceases before the healing occurs, so do not stop ministering if the person stops shaking or sits up.

9. Continually offer encouragement and help the person to

relax. Talk of the presence, power and promises of God. Explain that God is the healing God and that he has been healing people throughout history in a wide variety of ways. Suggest a relevant scriptural healing story for the person to read.

10. Maintain a flow of ministry between yourself, your partner, God and the person you are seeking to help. While one speaks aloud, the others can listen to God, pray silently for guidance, and watch the person being healed. The lead should pass from one to another as the Spirit prompts and common sense directs.

11. Silently use the gift of tongues. If you are unsure what to do next – or seem to be 'stuck' – it may be helpful to use the gift audibly. Explain what you are about to do with words like this: 'God has given me a language to use in prayer when I do not know how to pray. Neither of us will know exactly what I am praying, but be assured that it is the very best prayer I could possibly pray as God the Holy Spirit will be providing the words.'

12. Stop ministering when the person is healed, or when the Holy Spirit tells you to stop, or when you cannot think of anything else to do, or when the person asks you to stop, or when anyone appears tired. If the healing is incomplete, arrange to minister again in the near future, allowing time to elapse for further preparation and prayer.

These twelve suggestions may seem to presuppose that the healing will be a long drawn out affair rather than an instantaneous miracle as recorded in the New Testament. Of course, it is not always a lengthy process, but we do need to be ready to persist.

Some people have a real problem with this. 'Why the delay?' they say. 'Why the apparent half healings?' If we suggest these are due only to our sin or lack of faith it can seem as though we believe that we are personally involved in the mechanics of the healing. But God works the miracle. He brings the cure. We can only announce it.

Questioning people then ask why we have to go on announcing the cure. I think that there are many answers. For example, it is sometimes more important to God to heal our pride than to heal the other person's sickness; at other times, it is his priority to produce faith in us by developing our patience; and we must remember that many of our churches are rediscovering this ministry only after generations of neglect.

I believe that one of the central reasons for the delay is that, today, we mistakenly associate 'healing' with 'power'. We think God wants us to be powerful. We want to be powerful. We covet a 'power' ministry for ourselves and our church. And so God has to keep on reminding us that he does not want us to focus on our weakness, our ignorance and our vulnerability; he shows us that *his* strength and *his* power can be seen only when they are wrapped around human frailty and childlike simplicity. If we ache for God's name to be honoured mainly by instant, dramatic, sensational healings – with which *we* are seen to be involved – we need to reread 2 Corinthians 12:9–10 and learn from the apostle Paul.

In Part Two, we noted that after Jesus had healed someone, he often passed on his Father's advice, and this advice varied with different individuals. I suggest that we follow his example and offer whatever practical advice the Holy Spirit prompts us to give. He might, for example, ask us to mention some of the following matters.

1. The person could be encouraged to offer praise and thanksgiving. In Luke 17:11–19, Jesus added a spiritual blessing to the physical healing of the leper who returned with praise and thanksgiving. The person can be encouraged to do this as a daily affirmation, for every day free from pain or disability is a day of special blessing.

2. When drugs have been prescribed, or special medical care has been given, the person should be urged to visit the doctor for the healing to be verified. Medication should continue to be taken until the doctor has given permission to stop taking the drugs. In Matthew 8:1–4, Jesus encouraged the leper to visit the priests, partly to make the right thank offering under the Law, but also so that the healing could be verified and he could return to normal society.

3. It is always helpful to point the person towards the next step in Christian commitment – whether repentance, baptism, receiving the Spirit, or joining a church. Whenever people are

not believers, it is right to explain the good news and introduce them personally to the healing God.

4. If the cause of the ailment was sin, or if there was a demonic element, it may be right for this to be recognised and renounced by the person. Pray together about the matter and help the person to do this.

5. Further ministry will sometimes be necessary. Explain this and make plans for more ministry.

6. It is important to pray for the person's continuing healing, safety and protection. The enemy has been defeated, but must be expected to fight back.

7. Remember that Christ occasionally commanded silence, so do not automatically suggest that the person testifies about the healing. However, most of the people Jesus asked to keep quiet were so excited that they ignored his request and went about telling everyone! The desire to testify is a natural human response to good news, and most people will be encouraged by telling their friends about what God has done in their life.

# 18

# HEALING CONTEXTS

We saw in Part Two that Jesus and the early church leaders did heal during public worship, but that it was more common for them to heal in other contexts – either pastoral, evangelistic or informal gatherings of very sick people. In recent years, large numbers of British churches have introduced special healing services and regular times of ministry during their meetings. God has blessed these occasions, and has used them to encourage divine healing, but they are only one aspect of the restoration of the healing ministry rather than its complete format.

The great advantage of healing services and ministry times is that they bring the ministry of healing right into the centre of a local church's life. They make it plain to everyone that healing is very important, that we worship a healing God, and that supernatural principles run throughout our faith.

One disadvantage is that, unless great care is taken, healing services can suggest that the ministry rests in the hands of the leaders or the ordained. It seems to me that the gift of healing referred to in 1 Corinthians 12:9 does not reside in any one individual. As with all the 1 Corinthians 12 gifts, the gift of healing can be given by the Spirit to any believer in any service. It is suggested in 1 Corinthians 12:27–30 that a few people will be given this gift so regularly that it develops into a ministry, but these people will not necessarily be the elders or pastors.

At Kensington Temple, if one of the leaders senses that God wants to heal a person or an ailment, we always make room for this during the service. We also often have times of

195

general ministry at the end of services when our healing team is available to pray with sick people who have come hoping for a healing touch from God. I could fill this book with stories of people who have been healed by God in this way, but here are two simple illustrations of the way that God works in meetings.

One of our younger men had discovered three years earlier – when he was just sixteen – that he had a heart problem. He suffered chest pains whenever he climbed stairs, walked quickly or took any form of mild exercise. He became a Christian, learnt about God's healing, and often went forward for healing at meetings – but there had been no change in his condition. One Sunday in 1996, at one of our meetings, one of our pastors felt prompted to go to the young man during the service and tell him that he was healed. They prayed, but he felt nothing at the time. He realised that he had been healed only when he noticed that he could run, climb stairs and walk up slopes without any pain in his chest.

At a service in the summer of 1995, I sensed that God was wanting to heal someone with excruciating pain at the bottom of their back. I announced this, and a middle-aged lady came forward for prayer. She was suffering from a dislocated coccyx and a stomach problem, and was in such pain that she regularly visited an osteopath for treatment and had to take 300 tablets a month to control the pain. Her condition was so bad that she could not get into a bath or on to a bus, but she did not believe that she would ever be healed: she felt that there were many people in much greater need of healing than herself.

As we prayed for her, she felt a gentle heat go down her spine, and God completely healed her back and her stomach problem. She has been fully mobile and free from pain for over two years, and has not needed to take any more medication.

As healing has been given a higher priority in our church life, so we have found that some people have been healed during our services without any public ministry at all. For example, in October 1996, one of our members was involved in a serious motorcycle accident. His right knee was badly injured and he was told by the hospital staff that he would experience severe pain and a bad limp for several months. Two

196

weeks after the accident, however, all the pain suddenly disappeared during a time of worship and praise. He found that his limp had gone and that he had made an immediate and complete recovery.

Another member had for many years suffered from permanent and increasing pain in her knees and shoulders. At the beginning of 1997, during one of our services, she too was healed. I was simply reading a passage of Scripture to the congregation when she felt the power of God pass through her and remove her pain.

At other times, God seems to move in general healing power after our faith has been increased by a specific healing – perhaps after a very direct 'word of knowledge'. In January 1997, one of our young members started experiencing sharp pains in the lower part of her abdomen. Her doctor diagnosed a hernia, and told her that she would have to wait for it to drop before he could treat it. She became rather depressed when he told her that it could last many years.

She arrived an hour late at one of our midweek meetings, and insists that she 'was not in the mood' for a service. Just as she entered the church, the leader at that service announced that there was a wave of healing power passing through the people. Her pain left her instantly, and she has been fully pain free ever since.

*E*very church has its share of elderly, housebound saints, while at some point in their lives most believers are too ill to attend meetings. This means that we must make room in our thinking and ministry for the type of pastoral healing described in James 5:13–16. These verses are often mentioned generally in healing, but they have a particular pastoral application and are relevant only to the leaders or elders of a local church and to the sick people who are in a pastoral relationship with them.

These important verses encourage us to ask God for our own healing – to believe the healing promises and receive healing directly from the Lord – but they also ask us to present ourselves for pastoral healing.

It seems to me that this is the only section of the Church's healing ministry where leaders have exclusive authority. James 5:14 states, 'Is anyone among you sick? Let him call for the elders of the church; and let them pray over him, anointing him with oil in the name of the Lord.'

This does not authorise anointing with oil by those who are not elders or leaders, or the anointing of unbelievers. Instead, it indicates that believers who are ill – especially those who are still ill after praying for their own healing – should ask the elders to pray for them and anoint them with oil. This underlines the principle of partnership in healing which we considered earlier.

James 5:13–16 provides us with many valuable insights into pastoral healing. The simple question, 'Is anyone suffering?' reminds us that Christians are not exempt from the sufferings which come from the fallen world. Our victory in Christ is not about the absence of suffering, but about the way we handle trouble, conflict, suffering and pain.

James 5:13 prescribes the correct Christian response to suffering: 'Let him pray.' We are meant to *pray*, not to grumble, complain or feel bitter about our lot. And *we* are meant to pray – *we* have to find our own resource in God, not depend on the experience or testimony of others. This means that, when we are sick, we should first seek God for our own healing. We have seen in the Gospels how people approached Jesus with confidence and asked him to heal their diseases. In prayer, we do exactly the same thing and ask Yahweh Rapha to act according to his compassionate, unchanging nature.

Because of the cross, we can be healed by claiming the healing promises of God for ourselves. We do this by applying in prayer some of the truths and promises contained in passages like Psalm 38:3–10, 69:29–30, 103:1–4; Isaiah 40:27–31, 53:4–6; Ezekiel 47:1–12; and 1 Peter 2:24–25, as well as by applying lessons from the healing stories and the biblical principles we have examined throughout this book.

If the sickness persists, however, we are not left on our own. James 5:14 tells us that we should then call for the help of the pastoral leaders in our congregation so that they can minister to us – which must mean that healing is part of the pastoral ministry.

I suggest that two or three elders should pray with the sick person – the word 'over' shows that they have a God-given spiritual authority to pray for the sick in a pastoral setting. Their prayers should be offered in faith, in the knowledge of God's willingness to heal. James 5 teaches that the prayer of faith will heal the sick. The Greek word here for 'heal' is the same common Greek word which is used throughout the New Testament for both 'heal' and 'save', and this reminds us again that healing is one aspect of God's wider work of salvation in our lives.

Then the elders should pour a small amount of oil on the sick person's head while speaking some relevant words, for example, 'We anoint you with this oil in the name of Jesus Christ, that you may receive the anointing of the Holy Spirit to heal your sickness.' Some leaders anoint both the head and the hands to stress that the healing of believers should result in Christian service.

In the Scriptures, oil appears as a symbol of the Holy Spirit – and of healing, comfort, beauty, joy, humble service and caring devotion. All this points to a pastoral context of healing. I find it interesting that in biblical days shepherds applied olive oil to their sheep to keep flies and other insects away from their eyes so that they would be protected from disease. It seems that spiritual anointing by spiritual shepherds follows this natural pattern.

The word which James uses in this passage for anointing is not the same word which is used elsewhere in the Bible for the anointing with the Holy Spirit. It is a word which is used for more common and repeated anointings, and shows that this type of healing anointing is restorative and repeatable as the need arises.

James 5:15 reminds us that it is not the oil which heals, nor the prayers of the elders, nor the faith of the believer – it is the Lord who will raise up the sick person. It is too easy for us to become so preoccupied with healing techniques and ideas that we forget the simple truth that it is Yahweh Rapha who heals. We do have to pray, we do have to anoint with oil, we do need to have faith – but it is God who heals. We are his active partners, but he supplies all the power.

Verse 15 also suggests that sin may be the cause of the sickness, and this can block the healing. Pastoral counselling is the solution to this, and elders have a special responsibility as representatives of the body of Christ to ensure that mutual confession takes place. The references to sins being forgiven in the context of healing show us again that God wants to reach beyond purely physical healings to touch our whole lives with his love and healing power.

Despite all the scriptural promises of healing to God's people, and all the biblical teaching about pastoral healing and healing during public worship, we must not forget that most divine healing is meant to be set in an evangelistic context. This is where the chief focus of the Church's healing ministry should always be.

In Mark 16:17–18, Jesus asserts: 'These signs will accompany those who believe: In my name . . . they will place their hands on sick people, and they will get well.' Every believer who has been anointed with the Holy Spirit should be available to God as a partner in healing. All readers of this book should be ready to place their hands on the ailing bodies of their friends, relations, colleagues and neighbours, and to announce the arrival of God's cure.

We should be regularly petitioning along the lines of Acts 4:29–30, and should be spending much time in silent listening – waiting for the divine initiative and instruction. When our unbelieving acquaintances are ill, our compassion and our evangelistic passion should send us to our knees asking God to heal them and declaring our willingness to go and introduce his healing – if he desires to use us.

Some of us are over-enthusiastic while others are too reticent. God wants the enthusiastic to minister only when he prompts, and the reticent to ensure that they do minister when he does prompt. God wants our availability, our attention, and our obedient action. When we sense a word of direction from God that points us to a sick unbeliever, we should ask him to show us the how, where and when of ministry.

Then we can contact the person to whom God is directing us, and can say something like this: 'You know that I am a

Christian. Ever since I heard that you were ill I have been praying for your recovery. You probably know that in the Bible Jesus often directly healed people. I know that today he normally uses doctors and nurses, but he still does heal people supernaturally – and I think that I have received an impression from God that this is what he wants to do for you. Would it be possible for a friend from church and me to come and see you tomorrow afternoon? We would like to pray with you and bring you God's healing.' When we are polite, but firm and full of faith, we are rarely refused.

God's prompting will sometimes be so urgent that we are called to minister his healing in the street, on a bus or train, in a cafe or laundrette. I promise you, we have nothing to lose except our reputations: the person will not get worse through our praying, and might at once recover completely. You will not know unless you act. And if you obey the Spirit's prompting with sensitivity, gentleness, love and compassion, then the gift of your time and attention will in itself be therapeutic. The message that God cares will take root and begin to grow.

# 19

# HOPE FOR THE UNHEALED

*W*e have seen that Jesus healed everybody who came to him requesting healing, and that he cured all those to whom the Father sent him. But the rest of the New Testament is not a record of unbroken success. There are at least four references which may imply either unsuccessful or unattempted ministry for healing.

In 2 Timothy 4:20, Paul sadly records, 'But Trophimus I have left in Miletus sick.' (Trophimus the Ephesian is mentioned twice in Acts as a trusted travelling companion of Paul.) In 1 Timothy 5:23, Paul does not instruct his protégé Timothy to pray or have hands laid on him. Instead he urges him to 'no longer drink only water, but use a little wine for your stomach's sake and your frequent infirmities'. Paul may have been writing about a personal ailment in Galatians 4:13–14, 'You know that because of physical infirmity I preached the gospel to you at the first. And my trial which was in my flesh you did not despise or reject.' Finally, in Philippians 2:27, Paul records that the messenger Epaphroditus, 'was sick almost unto death; but God had mercy on him'. Does this mean that Epaphroditus was miraculously healed, or is a slow, natural recovery a more likely explanation?

It is interesting to note that these four sick men were all servants of God, and that Paul does not record any reason for their lack of healing. Their stories should be some small solace to us when we are faced with similar situations.

*D*isappointment is bound – at times – to face those of us who commit ourselves to the ministry of healing. There will be some people who are not healed, others whose initial healing lapses, and a few who are half healed and then make no further progress. There are many questions about this puzzle, and few answers in this life.

Sometimes, as I have suggested, the cure of our pride will be higher on God's agenda than the healing of the person's disease. In other instances, we will mishear God: there are bound to be a few occasions when we act out of human enthusiasm or because of worldly pressure. And there will be times when we have not prayed enough or have been distracted by materialism or unnecessary worries.

We might have been ambitious, impatient or fascinated by spiritual phenomena. We might have been concerned to stay safe in a narrow tradition or have experimented with unbiblical matters. We might have given up after a setback, exaggerated with false claims, or – worst of all – we might have blamed the sick person for the failure and have pretended that sin or lack of faith was the reason for the disappointment. Blame God, if you must. Blame the devil, if that is what you really believe. Blame yourself, if you have to. But never, ever blame the sick person.

All too often, believers who are involved in the healing ministry imply – either by innuendo or silence, or because they are embarrassed – that the failure is somehow the responsibility of the one they have prayed for rather than theirs. They hint that the person did not have enough faith, or was perhaps a little bit rebellious, or maybe did not really want to be completely healed. All of these are theoretical possibilities, but they are rarely the truth.

In one sense, it can never be right to say that nothing has happened. With God *nothing* is impossible; so if we have spoken his words, radiated his love, and performed his actions, something must have taken place. The gifts of our time and attention, our words and gestures, our prayers and practical caring all have healing value. This does not ignore the question of why physical healing has not taken place, rather, it negates the pretence that nothing has happened.

Sometimes, as with many of the Old Testament stories we examined in Part Two, the appreciation of the healing is delayed. At other times, the actual healing is gradual – as with Naaman, the Shunammitess' son, and the blind man in Mark 8. In cases like these there is no scriptural authority for suggesting that people should be urged to 'believe' God for a fuller healing than they are actually experiencing. The participants in these stories were not urged to intensify or quicken the healing by praise or belief. They were simply asked to obey God.

'Believism' is pretending, or trying to believe, that we are healed. Real faith is something quite different. Matthew 13:58 informs us that Jesus did not work many miracles in Nazareth because of the general lack of faith, but it does not say that he tried to work miracles and failed. The Scriptures do suggest that Jesus found the presence of faith in some people to be quite remarkable. There is no record, however, that Christ ever informed people that they could not be healed because they lacked faith or belief – though he did explain to the disciples that their lack of faith was preventing a boy from being healed.

The mere fact that a person comes to Christ requesting healing demonstrates faith. We do not need to imagine the person into being cured, or even to be thoroughly convinced ourselves that healing will take place, or to urge anyone to manufacture healing through spiritual will-power. We are only called to speak God's words, to perform his actions, and to be full of his overwhelming willingness to heal.

The truth is that people are sometimes not healed when we are absolutely certain that they will be, and that they may be healed when we are full of doubt and uncertainty. Unfortunately, we can never eliminate some degree of mystery from divine healing!

Some people turn to the Christian healing ministry only when a loved one is dying, and then see death as a failure. But, for believers, death is always the full and perfect healing, and those who are involved in this ministry must have an ʾequate theology of death. We must celebrate the fact that ʾst is as active in our dying as he is in healing, and that ʾan be miraculous deaths as well as wonderful cures!

In the early chapters of Part Three, we thought about the fulfilment of healing, the total transformation, which will take place at the day of resurrection. We saw that, somehow, we need to find the right balance between insisting that God does heal today and pointing people to the promised healing still to come. This means that we can look sick believers straight in the eye and promise them that they will be wonderfully healed. We can issue them with an unconditional guarantee that their pain and suffering will cease and that their broken body will be transformed. We do not always know when they will be healed, but we know that they will be.

In Christ, there is unlimited hope for healing – both now and in the future – and we need to encourage people to embrace every element of divine healing. They might not be healed now in the way that they hope, but they can be certain that – in Christ and because of the cross – they will be.

We must, however, be careful how we urge people to receive God's healing. There are many disabled people today who avoid Pentecostal and charismatic churches because of the insensitive treatment that they have received. I know that the Bible refers to 'the blind', 'the deaf' and 'the lame', but it is completely unacceptable for us today to personify people by their disabilities in this way. Laura is Laura. She's special and valuable and unique. She may have cerebral palsy, and she may need special, individual care, but she does not need every passing saint to stop and lay hands on her for healing – as though this is the only thing that matters for a person with a disability.

It is just not good enough for Christians to be eager to pray for people in wheelchairs but unwilling to install the slopes and special facilities they need. If our ministry of healing means that we genuinely care for 'the disabled', we will get involved in disability issues. We will help them on their terms and in the way that they seek; we will not presume that we know what they need or want. Some disabled groups campaign outside Christian healing meetings under the slogan, 'Rights, not miracles'. I often want to stand with them with Laura and our family banner – 'Rights *and* miracles'!

Some believers seem to be in greater need of emotional healing than the disabled are of physical healing, and we need to have a healing attitude which does not make people feel conspicuous, uncomfortable or unaccepted in their disability. We should not automatically assume that they are aching for physical healing, or that they lead lives which are unfulfilled. Please remember that a person who is physically or mentally handicapped is as much in God's image as a talented gymnast or a gifted dancer. We must respect each person's individual humanity and value the special contribution each person can make, but we must also sensitively encourage everyone to look to the loving hands of Yahweh Rapha.

It would be easy in a book like this to give the impression that every person I have ever prayed for has always been instantly healed, or that the healing ministry at Kensington Temple is the greatest thing since the book of Acts. God has been gracious, and I have seen him work in quite wonderful ways, but I always return home and weep about the multitude of sick folk who have not received their healing. By writing about my daughter, I have tried to show that my partnership with God is rooted in pain, and in a daily domestic struggle with the practical issues of disability and hardship. I know what it feels like to face disappointment and to be bewildered by God's sovereignty.

So it is from my experience in the whole area of helping the unhealed that I make the following suggestions of things that we can say and do when – after much ministry – an expected cure has still not taken place. As with the other suggestions I have made, please do not follow these slavishly – ask the Spirit to shape them to your own situation.

1. Have a prayerful de-briefing with your team and go through the steps you took in ministry. Try and find out whether you were obedient to every prompting. Establish if you made any mistakes or omissions.

2. Talk and pray about the whole matter with somebody who is more experienced than you in the healing ministry, and ask for suggestions. If anything emerges from the process

of de-briefing and seeking advice, arrange to see the person you ministered to again.

3. Pray and fast for guidance on your own. Ask God why the person was not healed.

4. Praise God with the person for the time of fellowship and prayer that you spent together. Point out that they are no worse off than before the prayer, and help them to appreciate the care and love of the people around. Remind them that the healing God is with them and cares for them.

5. Establish one thing that you have learnt from the episode and explain it to the person. Find out what the sick person learnt through the ministry, and praise God together for the insight. If other people were healed, encourage the person to praise God for the healings instead of wondering why they were not healed.

6. If the person you were ministering to is a Christian, encourage them to join you, or somebody else, in healing prayer for others. Point out that Elijah was healed of his depression by carrying out the three tasks he was given to perform.

7. Remind yourself that you are part of a battle, that the enemy is implacably opposed to healing, but that he has been defeated on the cross and will be destroyed at the last day.

8. Make sure that neither you nor the person feels guilty about the lack of healing. Explain that God's priority is often to prune the healing partner's reputation and pride – and laugh together about this.

9. Remind the person that Jesus' main purpose in super-natural healing is to point people to the reality of the kingdom rather than to give them a few more healthy years on earth. Show that Jesus does care about our bodies, but that he is more concerned about our eternal health and our full salvation. Encourage the person to take one more step towards God.

10. Send a short note thanking the sick person for giving the time, promising your continued prayers for healing, and suggesting something helpful to read from the Scriptures. Encourage the person to meditate on God's biblical healing promises and to apply them.

Some people, especially new Christians, do not know how

biblical promises, and it may be useful to indicate a
applying God's words. For example, a man suffering
say, asthma, could use Matthew 8:2–3 in the following
way.

He could be asked to sit quietly and to read the simple story
several times. He could then be encouraged to imagine the
scene, and to 'see' the leper coming to Jesus and being
cleansed. Next, he could personalise the story by applying it
to himself in this way: 'And behold, I came and worshipped
Jesus, saying, "Lord, if you are willing, you can make me
whole." Then Jesus put out his hand and touched me, saying,
"I am willing, be made whole." And immediately my asthma
was healed.' Finally, he can thank Yahweh Rapha for being
with him and for guaranteeing his healing. This is, however,
only one way of personalising God's word and it is not a healing
technique.

The Bible is packed with promises, and we can help people
to apply all of them in a similar way. The references to many
of these were given in Part Two, but we can also encourage
people to use some of these verses: Exodus 15:26; Deuteronomy 5:33, 7:15; 2 Chronicles 30:20; Job 5:26; Psalm 23:1–
2, 34:19–20, 41:3, 91:10–16, 103:1–3, 107:20, 116:8, 145:14,
146:8, 147:3; Proverbs 3:7–10, 4:20–23, 9:10–11, 16:24,
17:22; Isaiah 32:3, 35:5, 40:31, 41:10, 53:4–5, 58:8; Jeremiah
17:14, 30:17, Ezekiel 16:6; Hosea 13:14; Matthew 10:1,
11:4–5; Romans 8:11, 32; 1 Thessalonians 5:23; 2 Timothy
1:7; Hebrews 12:12–13, 13:8; 1 John 3:8; 3 John 1:2; and
Revelation 22:1–4.

Although we should urge people to go on praying for their
healing, and to go on claiming God's promises for healing,
we should not neglect to remind them to be hungrier for the
healer than for their healing. We have to recognise that,
ultimately, healing is not the great hope of the unhealed. Jesus
is. In the middle of all our pain and problems, all our
disappointments and difficulties, our only hope of inner peace
and contentment is to keep our attention tightly focused on
Jesus, and on his overwhelming love for us. He is the only
rock which will stand when everything else collapses around
us.

If we are preoccupied with healing, we will never be whole and we will never know peace. But if our goal is God himself, we will find that Yahweh Rapha soon embraces us in his gentle healing arms.

# 20

# HOPE FOR THE HURTING

The Christian men and women who develop fruitful healing ministries are the ones who persist through the barren months, who go on responding to the requests of hurting people and the Spirit's quiet instructions – even when their personal experience suggests that they are wasting their time.

After our reputations and pride have been buried, God in his grace sends his resurrection power. We cease trying, stop shouting, suspend the techniques that we borrowed from somebody else, and start watching Christ heal the sick through us. Healing can be an exciting thrill for those who have not passed through the school of pain; but to those who have graduated with crucifixion honours, the Christian ministry of healing is a deeply humbling experience.

Believers seeking to minister in healing sometimes find that God seems to heal in waves of power. For a few weeks or months, it seems that everybody they pray for is healed. Then, for a while, with no obvious explanation, hardly anybody appears to be healed. Later, suddenly, it all happens again. This may have been Paul's experience in Acts 16–20, and it has been repeated throughout history in the lives of some whom God has greatly used in healing.

God plunged me in at the deep end at Nyota Farm, and gave me a genuine taste of revival. But I then passed through a long time of learning and longing. Since then, he has been blessing our work in a remarkable way, which – at times – has even outshone the events in Kenya. The barren times should not be filled with agonised searching for hidden sins or some other cause, instead they should be full of relevant effective,

Pentecostal evangelism; simple, uncluttered, holy living; and fervent prayer for God to work again in great power.

In nearly every section of the Church, on every continent around the world, the Spirit has re-quickened a zeal for healing. So too has the devil. In Part Three, we saw that demonic diagnosis and pagan healing are starting to proliferate in western Europe. This should not surprise us, as Revelation 13 foretells that this will be so in the last days. But as more and more hurting people are turning to alternative medicine, and are increasingly open to spiritual cures, we need to be those who will stand up with integrity and announce that Yahweh Rapha is among them, that the healing kingdom has come.

And it has come. The healing God is with us. People are being made whole. In the divine healing ministry, we are not peddling illusions to gullible people, or pretending that emotional experiences are physical improvements. We are reminding people about God's promises, we are passing on what he is saying, we are reporting what he is doing. He honestly is healing men and women. There is real hope for hurting people. It is genuine, tangible and true.

For three years, a young woman had suffered from a form of obsessive dieting which was classified as an 'Obsessive Compulsive Disorder' – often considered to be incurable. At the beginning of 1996, her dieting became the worst that it had ever been and her weight plummeted. She was placed on medication and given exercises, but there was no improvement.

One night, when finally she could stand it no longer, she knelt by her bed in despair and cried out to God. She knew that without his divine help she would soon kill herself. At that moment, she felt as though Jesus had come down to sit on her bed, and that he was gently holding her head in his lap. She experienced complete peace. She did not know that she was being cured, but a few days later she noticed that the condition and anxiety had completely disappeared. She has remained fully healed ever since – and, not surprisingly, is now a devoted follower of Christ.

A journalist had suffered from severe breathing difficulties

211

for many years, and was eventually diagnosed as having acute bronchial asthma. Her condition deteriorated throughout 1995 until in October she collapsed and was rushed to hospital. She continued to worsen and it seemed as though she was going to die.

At the lowest point, she turned to the Bible and read Romans 8:11, 'If the Spirit of him who raised Jesus from the dead dwells in you, he who raised Christ from the dead will also give life to your mortal bodies through his Spirit who dwells in you.' She had been a church attender for many years, but suddenly saw this verse in a new way. She was convinced that it was God's word to her for healing, and she claimed the promise for her condition. The healing God reached out to her, kept his wonderful promise, and she has not had to visit a doctor or hospital since.

True stories like these provide the hope that hurting people need. The queues in a GP's waiting room do not exist because the people know that the doctor will guarantee a cure, for some patients visit their doctors knowing there is a good chance that they will not be helped. Instead, they go to their local surgery because some people are helped and they hope it will be their turn that week.

But, in Christ, it is always our turn. His promises are absolute. Sickness – the fruit of sin – has been defeated. Healing and wholeness are before us. Yahweh Rapha is with us. There is enough hope in God for all the world's hurting people, and increasing numbers of people are embracing it.

We are all surrounded by hurting people, by men and women who are troubled by divorce, unemployment, addictions, debt, loneliness, sickness, poor health and all the worries and stress of modern-day life. Because of this, now surely must be the time for you to start partnering God and begin taking his wholeness to some of the needy people near you.

You probably have a burden for one or two particular people who are struggling with an ailment or sickness, and you now realise that God has been directing you to them through the burden. You have always longed to reach out and help them.

You have always been able to imagine what would happen if Jesus should meet them. Now you know that God wants you to take his healing and wholeness to them. Please do it. Please respond to the Spirit's prompting with willing obedience. For these people, you are the embodiment of the hope that they are seeking.

Deep down, you know that your Christian life should be different. You know that Jesus lives and acts and heals today through his anointed disciples on earth. You understand that the Holy Spirit has been poured on to you so that you can share Jesus' power and authority. You know that the Spirit's anointing on your life should make a dynamic healing difference to the people around you. Please let it be so.

I have written this book because I am convinced that God wants to use *you* to take his healing and wholeness to some of the sick people around you. I know this because he is using thousands of ordinary people in this way in the churches I lead in London. They are his healing partners, and – with God's help – they are making a real difference.

Sadly, there are some people who are so stuck in spiritual ineffectiveness that they assume their condition is normal. They think that nothing can ever change. You know this is not true for you. As you have read this book, you have felt God warming your heart and breathing expectancy into your spirit. You suspect that God has led you to this book for a purpose, so please start to prepare yourself spiritually to begin co-operating with God in his great healing work.

My main prayer for you is that you will submit yourself completely to the work of the Spirit in your life. This will not be something which happens by accident. God will not make you submit to him. You must decide to partner him. It has to be a conscious act of your will – one that you go on making every day of your life.

We are all called to become true partners with the Spirit in God's work. Our part is to provide the hands and voice, his part is to direct and enable. We cannot control or manipulate God, for he works through us and he uses us. But he does not do this mechanically, overriding our free will. We have to co-operate with him as a genuine partner in the task of taking God's healing love to a hurting world. I ask you, please open yourself fully to him and start to do this.

The broken-hearted lives you know, the damaged people you pass on the streets, your bruised neighbours and friends, the sick people in your area: these people may not realise it just yet, but they all are waiting to be healed by the loving power of God.

Jesus is looking for men and women who will turn away from human reasoning and worldly methods. He is seeking believers who will live in complete dependence on the Holy Spirit and total obedience to his promptings. He wants you. He wants you to live for him, to minister with him. Jesus is calling you now to share his healing life and ministry.

I believe that it has never been more important than it is today for Christians to crucify their reputations, to trust the foolishness of God, and to be ready to touch the sick and speak God's words of healing. I am equally sure that it has never been so critical for the Church to offer the disciples' prayer to God: 'Help your servants to proclaim your word with all boldness, by stretching out your hand to heal and to work signs and wonders through the name of your holy servant Jesus.'

Our healing God wants an army of obedient servants who will echo his healing voice and be his holy hands. It is my sincere prayer that you will volunteer for Christ's healing ministry, and that you will learn both how to receive healing for yourself and also how to minister it to others. God only desires your availability: give him that, and one day soon he will use you in a miracle.